Praise for
Meister Eckhart's Book of Darkness & Light

"Sweeney and Burrows, in poems that are as elegant as they are scholarly, revoice Meister Eckhart's grounding and expansive instructions to 'seek the light that shines / out of the darkness.'"

—Pádraig Ó Tuama, poet and host of
Poetry Unbound, from On Being Studios

"Meister Eckhart is one of the greatest of Christian mystics, but because of his depth, he can be challenging to read. Jon M. Sweeney and Mark S. Burrows unlock the poetry in his words to allow his light to shine. What Coleman Barks has done for Rumi, they have done for Eckhart—making his insight accessible and his wisdom sing."

—Carl McColman, author of
The New Big Book of Christian Mysticism and *Eternal Heart*

"Each poem is short, spare, distilled. And each one is footnoted, so the reader might begin in enchantment, then trace the poetry to its source. A sure-footed path toward mastering one of the great masters of the last millennia."

—*The Chicago Tribune*

"Those who cherish the spiritual verse of Rumi, Hafiz, Kabir, and other ecstatic poets will gladly commune with Eckhart and his reverence for the mysteries of life. A 'Best Spiritual Book of 2019.'"

—*SpiritualityandPractice.com*

"Positioned as a follow-up to *Meister Eckhart's Book of the Heart*, this book by collaborators Sweeney and Burrows collects meditations from the 14th-century priest and mystic…. Eckhart's mystical musings lead toward an 'undoing, letting go of our need to manage our lives, freeing ourselves to seek this treasure.' VERDICT: with an economy of language, these words read like Buddhist koans, encouraging a path toward the richness of an interior life."

—*Library Journal*

Meister Eckhart's Book of
Darkness & Light

Meditations on the Path of the Wayless Way

JON M. SWEENEY AND **MARK S. BURROWS**

HAMPTON ROADS

Cover art "Thrush" © Lisa Graa Jensen.
All rights reserved 2022 / Bridgeman Images
Typeset in Truesdell

Hampton Roads Publishing Company, Inc.
Charlottesville, VA 22906
Distributed by Red Wheel/Weiser, LLC
www.redwheelweiser.com

ISBN: 978-1-64297-045-6

Library of Congress Cataloging-in-Publication Data

Names: Sweeney, Jon M., 1967- editor. | Burrows, Mark S., 1955- editor.
Title: Meister Eckhart's book of darkness and light : meditations on the path of the wayless way
/ Jon M. Sweeney and Mark S. Burrows. Description: Charlottesville, VA : Hampton Roads
Publishing, [2023] | Summary: "Meister Eckhart has been a huge influence on spirituality for
more than 800 years. This book of meditations is for people seeking the 'wayless way.' It is not for
those looking for a simple path. These fresh, stunning renderings of Eckhart's writings in poetic
form bring life to one of the great spiritual voices of any age. They reveal what it means to love
God and find meaning in darkness-not darkness in   general, but your darkness. Only when you
are in the darkness, Meister says, do you have even the possibility of seeing the light"-- Provided
by publisher. Identifiers: LCCN 2022042748 | ISBN 9781642970456 (paperback) | ISBN
9781612834832 (kindle edition) Subjects: LCSH: Eckhart, Meister, -1327. | Mysticism. |
BISAC: RELIGION /   Mysticism | POETRY / Subjects & Themes / Inspirational & Religious
Classification: LCC B765.E34 M455 2023 | DDC 189/.5--dc23/eng/20221209
LC record available at *https://lccn.loc.gov/2022042748*

Printed in the United States of America
IBI
10 9 8 7 6 5 4 3 2

CONTENTS

*Know this: God has imprinted God's image within you, and nothing
you do and nothing that happens to you can erase this beauty,
which is with you even when you ignore or betray it.*

⁝

*Within each of us is a divine treasure, and if we hope to discover it
we need to go deep into the heart of who we are.*

⁝

*To find that treasure requires that we work like a wood carver
who does not work by adding but by cutting away,
removing what is rough to reveal
what shimmers from within.*

⁝

*Those who know nothing other than creatures need no sermon,
for each creature is full of God and is a book.*

—MEISTER ECKHART

INTRODUCTION

The eye with which I see God is exactly the same eye
with which God sees me.
My eye and God's eye are one eye:
one seeing, one knowing, one loving.
—MEISTER ECKHART

I f you have ever wondered what it might be to set out on a "way-less way," this book might be for you. Many in our time want something else. They want a straight path toward a defined goal. They desire one without detours, led by a guide who tells them exactly what to do. And what not to do. Especially the latter. They want to know what they should think, and feel. They need to know where they should go—and not go. Especially that.

Fundamentalists are always among us, because many want easy answers and cheap trips. Ones that don't call us to face difficult choices. Or hard decisions. Ones that avoid tough thinking. "Just tell me what I need to do," they say. And bit by bit, they become less and less free, and more and more stupefied, until finally they have no voice of their own. No character to stand upon. And no will to resist the tyranny that started out as their choice. If you find yourself in that description, this is not the book for you.

But if you have wondered whether one could still "think God" in such days as these, without relinquishing one's brain, stay with us here. If you can imagine what it might mean to set out on a "wayless way," not one mapped by tired orthodoxies or mindless strategies, then Eckhart might be the Meister—or "master"—you have been looking for. Perhaps even the one you deserve. And surely one of the ones you need. But try this out for size before reading further. Imagine wandering into a house of worship and hearing someone telling you to "take leave of God for the sake of God." Or that "all things are equal and alike in God and are God." What would you make of claims like these? Everything is God? Everything? Really?

If such thoughts strike you as absurd, you are surely right in saying so. But perhaps absurdity—as Eckhart knew—is the only way forward in difficult times, something he knew since the word "absurdus" in the Latin of his day meant "to be out of tune," even "silly." And in an "out-of-tune" culture—like his . . . and ours—how else should we seek a way forward than by tilting things inside out? For to be absurd in sane times might be foolish, but to be foolish in foolish times might just be a mark of wisdom. As it was for Eckhart in his day. And might well be in ours as well.

Who was this man, Eckhart, who entered the Dominican Order as a young man and rose to eminence as a celebrated—if controversial—preacher and teacher? A friar who came from the Germanic territory known as Thüringen, Eckhart became widely revered as a scholar, teacher, and preacher and distinguished himself in service to his order. His fame led to his being known simply by his academic title, Meister, the highest degree given in universities of his day. He was an adventurous thinker whose radical formulations worried some in positions of authority who accused him late in his life of holding heretical views. Others have come to see him as a mystical thinker, a prophetic voice who refused to be satisfied with conventional views. In any case, he was a daring intellectual and a compelling preacher who devoted himself to finding new ways to imagine and express the divine mystery, often relying on paradox and a newly invented vocabulary.

With thinking like this, of course, it is no wonder Eckhart was charged with heresy. Some of those in positions of power within the church feared him as a prophet who dared to think new thoughts, not by seeking different orthodoxies or alternative paths, but by imagining we could live by turning toward "a wayless way." One that cannot be mapped. Because the Meister knew that only original thoughts, even absurd thoughts, have the power of startling us into new vision. Only paradox and contradiction can free us for new ways of thinking and freer ways of living. "Wayless ways," as it were. Which he knew was what we yearn for in the depths of our souls.

What is it to speak of a wayless way, as Eckhart did? What is it he's onto with such a metaphor? Such a way is one that cannot be mapped. That resists premature certainties. That is open for what you cannot expect, perhaps even for what you did not desire. Because following those ways leaves you only with what you already knew, and consigns you to stay where you already were—looking backwards into your past, and not forward into your future. Which is what something deep within us desires, even when we fear it. So it is that he insisted that we must "renounce God for the sake of God," discovering in that renunciation the freedom to experience "a single oneness" by which we are "one with God" and not simply "united."

How do we make progress on this journey into "oneness?" For progress is what Eckhart was all about. To answer this question, only paradox, only what seems absurd, will do: "Possessing nothing, being naked, poor and empty, transforms nature," he writes. Do you get this? If so, perhaps you are kidding yourself. Because it is not your purpose, he might say, simply to get this—or to get this simply. Your purpose is to be grasped by this truth, to open yourself to be "gotten" by it, so that it begins to turn your life upside down. This is the "breakthrough"—a word Eckhart coined—into life lived on "a wayless way."

Perhaps, when that begins to happen, you will start to see that the purpose of your life is not to find some map to tell you where to go, but to see that your deepest longing is to catch a glimpse, at least, of how you are to go—whatever your path. Understanding this is the first step toward finding the joy of being on the wayless way. Which is nowhere and everywhere, and always where you are. Here and now. Setting forth on this path does not require more baggage than you have when you are empty-handed. What you need is to relinquish what you thought you needed—and who you thought you were. What you need is the wisdom to let go of your expectations of yourself, of others, and yes, of God. What you need is the courage to get up, if you have fallen. And, once you are standing on your own feet, to turn around, so that the way ahead of you leads into your future. Which is absurd. And yet the one truth you need to find your way.

Eckhart, you see, dared to refuse conventional thinking. He risked exposing orthodoxies if they only dulled the mind into submission. For him, the adventure awaiting each of us was and is to discover the freedom that is our birthright. And resist all that numbs us into rigidity. For this reason, he delighted in contradiction and reveled in paradox, that most subversive and freeing way of thinking. Because only by subverting foolish thinking can you begin to get your proper bearings in this life. In your life.

You might have guessed that Eckhart did not suffer fools lightly. Because he knew that setting out on the wayless way would require that you renounce your most deeply cherished thoughts—about yourself, about God, about others—if these prove to be false. Even if they belong to the comfortable certainties you've staked your life on. Or rather, especially in such a case.

In a culture that craved light—and what culture doesn't?—Eckhart dared to imagine that darkness is what matters most—and not the darkness in general, if there is such a thing, but *your* darkness. Because it is the one thing you know most about, and without it, you will never know who you are or what it means to desire the light. You will never imagine what light is all about—and that you always carry it within you. Always. Only when you are in the darkness, he wrote, do you have even the possibility of seeing the light.

He knew that in the darkness, and only in the darkness, will you know what it means to desire it. Just as you'll only know what it is to long for freedom when you realize how enchained you are—in your own wishful thinking and tepid imagining. Or in the thoughts of others that you've made your own. Even when they don't ring true for you. Finally, only the darkness, your darkness, will unsettle you from the untruths that keep you shackled, and open you to that "little spark," as he called it, that you always carry in the depths of your soul.

You see, Eckhart was a preacher. And when he preached, he did so as poets do: he spoke imaginatively, and delighted in metaphor. He preferred to show rather than tell. But he did so with a fierce intellectual prowess, as the best poets also know to do. He joins them in realizing that puzzlement matters. That we need to be startled out of our intellectual slumbers, which is one form of our darkness, if we hope to glimpse the light we always carry within us. Which we do, every one of us, despite our protests to the contrary. Each of us, somewhere in the depths of our hearts, desires to be "untroubled and unfettered by anything," he insists. Anything. And everything. Especially conventional beliefs with all their rigidities, together with premature certainties and wishful thinking, with all its flabbiness. All of which diminishes us.

In his own defense of the charges some in the church made against him, Eckhart explained that he wrote in "emphatic speech." Not the kind of emphatic that means raising the decibel level. But the kind that speaks with urgency and authenticity. The kind that refuses to be silenced into simplistic answers or petty docility. He loved questions, knowing that his hearers alone could find the answers they needed. Only as poets, he knew, could he—and we—reach for the truth that is always on the far side of speech—but on the near side of our minds. "When we live without a Why," he suggests, we come to be "born again into God." And by that he meant not once, as fundamentalists of every stripe—whether religious or secular—might say. But again . . . and again . . . and again.

This ongoing birthing is what it means, he suggests, to taste true freedom. The kind that disrupts our gloom, and invites us into more generous company. This, he insists—calling on language familiar to his hearers—is what it means to be "transformed in love." To become love. Again and again.

His preaching style was often unorthodox and always allergic to conventional thinking. Because that would never end well, he knew. It would always leave us languishing in stale thoughts—about the one we call God, about humanity, about the world, about our "self"—which no longer persuade the mind or convince the heart. Eckhart was if anything a daring thinker, one who knew to refuse clichés and oppose smugness. And he loved paradox, that most puzzling of thought-forms. Who but such a Meister could write, as he does in one of his sermons, that "heaven is cheap because it is on sale to everyone at the price they can afford!" and then add in the next breath that "we should therefore give all that we have for heaven, especially our own self-will!" Ah, the lure of paradox, which may be simple, but—as in this case—reaches the deep and freeing truths on a "wayless way," those that wait for us beneath the weight of our complexities and the false burden of our own importance.

Eckhart won't be the guide everyone in our day desires. Many will fear him, as they did in his own times. They will look for someone to comfort them—which he knew about but refused to do if it meant coddling his hearers into blind obedience. He recognized that we were made to reach higher—and deeper—than this. And he reached for something many long for in our day: a way that begins anywhere—and everywhere— which is to say, wherever and however and whoever we are. And one that has a destination that is never in this life final, that could be found anywhere and is finally to be discovered everywhere. Meaning this: live where you are. And there, risk living into the abundance of who you are, without looking for an escape into some fantasy or other, which is always dead-end thinking.

What you have to learn, again and again, and what Eckhart was intent on reminding you of, is that the only way forward is on the way of paradox. Which is a wayless way, the one that leads you, finally, into the wholeness of your life, beyond any way that avoids challenges or leads toward fixed destinations.

Thus, a word of caution: for those who want to know The Truth in some single, infallible way, or by following some unswerving method, stay far from Eckhart. There are preachers and guides enough who will sell you this fare for whatever you are willing to pay. But if you find yourself drawn to a guide, like Eckhart, who can tell you to "examine yourself, and wherever you find yourself, then take leave of yourself," then he might be the wise fool you have been looking for. Or at least the one you most need.

But if so, prepare yourself to live into paradox upon paradox, and puzzlement after puzzlement. Because only in the unsettling of this wayless way will the radiance of truth strike you with the power to rise from your darkness. One that will carry you into the light—but always by reminding you—by re-minding you—that you have always carried this light within yourself. As what he calls the "little spark," or Fünklein. Where should you look for it? Not here or there, in some place or other, but within you. Now, do you see?

If so, you probably know that advice is the last way to reach people—including you. Confusion might be a far better approach, since only by being puzzled can you begin to find new directions in which to think and live. To that end, he suggests that the only way to reach people was to speak in startling ways, to use metaphors that might seem like madness, because

"nothing else could adequately capture the truth [about God],"
as he put it.

So come along as we journey with Eckhart on the wayless
way he envisions, glimpsing the wonders of his "Book of Dark-
ness and Light." And trust that you will find not simply startle-
ment, but encouragement—"to live," as he once put it, "in a
way that the whole of [your] life is love." If you think such a
claim is ridiculous, you are right. But you might also know, or
intuit, that such a claim is not only true, but worth living for.
Only such a life is worth the sacrifice required. If something
in you says "Yes!" to his vision, even if it seems difficult, even
impossible, then come along and see what it means to aim for
such a goal, which is the wayless way that is freedom and light,
joy and delight.

Setting Forth Together

Let's be clear about one thing: you are
your own best teacher. I can only tell
you what I know, but you'll need to
discover it for yourself, so don't expect
me to tell you what to think or how to live.

I'll share with you the truth I've found:
that life is full of a darkness that can
enlighten you in its own way; there's
a thread there to guide you, but to find
it you'll need to look within yourself.

When you do, seek the light that shines
out of the darkness, and be radiant for
those who long for hope to brighten
their journey, setting forth together on
what you'll discover is a wayless way.

Part One

In the Beginning . . . Darkness

Want to Know How to Find God?

If you want to know how to find God,
there is no clearer way than
seeking him where it was
you last left him.
If you feel you cannot find God,
then retrace your steps.
You will surely come upon him there.

There Is a Light Within You

I've said many things, but at the heart
of them all is this: There is a light
within you, in your soul, uncreated
and uncreatable; it simply is.

If you wish to know yourself,
look for this light in the dark;
it is ever present, even when
you've lost sight of it. Look
away from what you think
you are, and look deeper into
the darkness that is within.

There you'll find that light
which is ever radiant,
even if no one—not
even you—notices.

Who You Are

This is both simple and not simple:
give your everything to God;

God will do with it, and with you,
what is perfect and true.

But you cannot, should not, worry
yourself about outcomes; God will

do what God will, with the nothing-
ness of your all. Trust in this;

the rest will follow.

The Darkness of Unknowing

If you wish to experience what it is
to be born anew, you must leave
the crowd and return to the source
where you began; there, beyond
all thought and imagination and
intention, there, in that darkness,
you will prepare yourself to be
born, shining forth with a stirring
that comes solely from within,
not from you but from God alone.
This birth begins in the darkness
of unknowing when you have
relinquished all that you understand;
only when you have abandoned
your knowing and willing can
God shine forth within you.
This is the noble birth.

Choose Darkness

Nothing can bring you to know God.
Well, not quite; there is something,
but it is an unknowing, a forgetting
of yourself, an utter emptying.
Someone heard me say this and asked,
Should I stand, then, in complete darkness?
I answered, Yes, that would be best!
You're never closer to God than when
you are in utter darkness and unknowing.

In puzzlement they asked, *But what is this darkness?*
What is it like? I told them this: What you call it
is unimportant; open in yourself a state of receptivity
and you will find it; it is the darkness described by
the prophet who said: *I will lead my beloved*
into the wilderness, and there I will speak to her heart.
Choose darkness, then; desire to be led into the wilderness
where you will lose your self, becoming pure nothingness;
there you will come to know true freedom.

The Dark Way

You can do no better than to place yourself
in darkness, no longer striving to know
and discover, but rather to un-know.

This is a sacred potential darkness, one
of possible receptivity where you will find
yourself in a position to be made whole.

Forgetfulness of self and other creatures
is the dark way of unknowing, and it is
the path of bare simplicity—to God.

Spoken in Solitude

The true test of your vow of simplicity,
barrenness, and abandonment is this:
that you would sing with David,
For a day in your courts is better
than a thousand elsewhere.

A word of eternity is uttered,
and heard, in solitude, where
you are a stranger to yourself
and others, but an intimate
of the Holy One.

Obedience

Doing the right thing
is never the best thing;
it's far better when you
open your heart in what-
ever it is you are doing.
This brings out the best
in all that is done, and
shines forth within you,
even in the darkness.

Tasting Freedom

Only when you let go of your self
do you start to become empty
enough so that God has
room to work in you;
so try going out of yourself
and letting go of what
you think is your own,
and taste the freedom of
being without wanting.

So You Can't Pray?

So you can't pray no matter
what you've tried? Then stop
trying and try to free your mind
of what you thought prayer was.
For this freedom is true prayer,
whether or not you are praying.

Trying to Pray Properly

Once you get used to not trying to pray
properly, imagine what it feels like

to be free of what you thought you
should be doing in the first place.

When you begin with this, you'll
find that every pore in your body

begins to pray with you.

What's the Best Way to Find God?

People often ask me if it's better
to flee from people and seek the quiet
of a church in order to find God.

I tell them this is the wrong way
to think. What you need is to be in
the right state of mind, regardless

of whom you're with or where you
are; if you have God, in the right mind,
you'll have God everywhere in your

life, no matter where you are or
whom you're with. How, you ask?
Intend God in everything you do

until it all becomes God for you.

God Cannot Resist

Many think that the best way is
to exalt themselves above others,
and take the finest seat at the feast.

I say it's better to abandon yourself
for the sake of God, refusing to
elevate yourself; ask rather to take

the lowest place, and when you do
God cannot resist pouring all that God
is—including divinity—into you.

Anything less than this would
mean that God was not God, which
cannot possibly be.

Where Darkness Takes You

How is this for darkness?
You are known
in heaven
without your
face and form
because there
is one image
only and it
is God in whom
you are truly seen.

This Is Your Life

So you think God should be shining forth
in your religious devotions and acts? Perhaps.
But think again. If you're in the right frame
of mind, you'll find that God is radiant in
everything, above all in what is dark
or seems far from God. Because nothing
is far from God; everything is always in
God. I'd even say that everything *is* God.
Coming to know this takes practice, and
you will never finish learning what this
means in your life—because this is your life.

The Restlessness of Peace

Some people think that the purpose of life
is to find rest, but I say this: if your heart
is grounded in God, you'll never be content
with being at rest; you'll always be striving
to find God in all that is, whatever it is you
are experiencing. And above all in things
that might seem alien or strange to you.
To seek this, in darkness, is higher than
attaining peace, because as you do, little
by little you'll find yourself grasping God
in everything that is, which is true freedom.

There Is No Why

I have often said that whenever
you seek God and find something,
you'll not find God unless you
seek without motive or reason.

So why should you seek God?
Simply because God, who has
no motive or reason, *is*.

Seek whylessly, then, and
all will be well, knowing
that there is no Why in
pursuing the Holy One.

Your Soul Has Two Faces

> Your soul has two faces,
> one gazing up at God
> and one angling down,
> to guide your senses.
> That upper soul-face
> is as if in eternity,
> not in this world,
> a light that shines
> with the burning brand
> of the Holy Ghost.
> Cultivate that face,
> and remember
> your gazing as
> you walk in this world.

Will to do the good

and when you do, you'll find that nothing
can disturb you; you won't always succeed
at it, but seeking to do it and desiring this
above all else is worth more than something
requiring little of you. For the act of desiring
something a thousand miles away is more
truly yours than what is lying in your lap
that you don't know about or want to have.

Your Desire Matters

If you want to do what is good
but lack the capacity to pull it off,
it's all the same to God, for your
desire matters. Why is this so?
Because your will expresses what
you desire to do, just as your desire
guides your will, shaping you in
the ways you are toward others,
and this matters—not only to God,
but to those you love, whether
or not they desire it.

Religion Can Be a Trap

Religion can be a trap, convincing us
that it's best if we experience ecstasy
in our prayer or devotions. But this
is wrong. If you've attained this and
meet a sick person who asks you for
a bowl of soup, it's better to leave
your ecstasy for the sake of love,
for only in this way will you know
what is more worthy than religion.

Go to the Desert

The desert is
where we hear
God.
I will draw her
into the wilderness,
and speak
tenderly to her,
our Lord says of
that gentle one,
quite poor and quiet,
who is prepared
to be alone,
one on One.

Choose Silence

Some think that they can speak about God.
But I say this: whatever you imagine in your
mind is wholly unlike what we call God.

Those who know this do not teach; they
even refuse to speak, preferring silence
to all else—even what might be true.

If you've glimpsed the hidden truth,
even for a moment, and found it in
the darkness of the mystery

beyond words, the only thing
to do is to choose
silence.

You Are Not Alone

However great your suffering might be,
remember this: let it pass through God,
trusting that God can endure it even
if it seems too great a burden to bear
on your own—because you are not alone.
Remember that only in the darkness can
you begin to see the light, which helps
only if you turn to take advantage of it.

When You Are Seeking God

When you are seeking God, seek not only
God but his will for you. God's deepest wish
is that we learn to want only what he wants.

Even a St. Paul, who spoke often with God,
and God with him—wouldn't that be nice—
amounted to nothing until he was able to say,

What do you want me to do, Lord? Hear me:
You will never be as true to yourself as you are
when you have given up your will to God.

An Even Greater Marvel

Is the greatest act you can imagine
God capable of doing that of making
a new creation all over again?
Yes, that would surely be a marvel,
but there is an even greater one:
that God befriended you in
the heart of your darkness,
embracing all of who you are—
what a miracle! How else would
you ever have known that even
you are capable of becoming
a new creation?

The Need for Penance

A body is often
too strong
for the spirit.
When there is
a fight going on
between body and soul,
the body easily wins;
it has so much on its side
here in this world.
Bodies are at home here,
rooted and fed and comforted.
Easy living makes a body
take it easy. But the soul
is in a strange place,
needing assistance to get
out from under that
soft belly.

God Is a God of the Present

So you feel remorse for what you've done
or failed to do? Remember that God is the God
of the present, and takes you as you now are,
and not as you once were.
If God holds no anger toward you,
and refuses to blame you, and doesn't
even remember your failings, who are you
to hold onto your shame?

Remind yourself that only in the depths
will you ever come to know the joy of being
lifted up to the heights, just as only the dark-
ness awakens you to savor the gift of light.

What Does God See?

When God gazes upon you,
what does God see? Not your
failings or your inadequacies,
and not your darkness. No,
God sees your suffering
and distress, and lets your
failures vanish more quickly
than you can blink an eye.

Lighten Your Load

Your sins are your problem, not God's.
Since love covers them over and knows
nothing of them, why do you hold onto
them? Listen to me: lighten your load!
Do you imagine you know who you are
and what you need better than God does?
Or do you think your sins are so important
that they're greater than God's forgiveness?
If so, think again.

A Perfect Equation

You can never love God too much,
just as God does not limit forgiveness,
and when you come to know this,
the only proper response is trust.
So do—trust; the rest will follow.

In Such Company

We are indistinct from the One
who is pure unity so that everything
that is in the One *is* the One.
Since this is true, when one suffers
who is fully present with God,
God is fully suffering too,
and when your pain and loss
are God's pain and loss,
you may not understand it
fully, but be grateful to be
in such good company.

Let God Be God in You

If God has redeemed the whole world,
who are you to think your sins are so special
that they are beyond God's embrace?
Flee, then, to the One in whom no fault
can be found, who finds nothing at all
to blame you for. Take pleasure in letting
God be God in you, gracing you as a treasure
without needing a reason or setting a measure.

God Waits at Your Door

Some folks think that their faults
or their weaknesses or something else
drive God far from them, but I
disagree with this. Even if you
push God out of the house, God
goes no further than the door
and will wait there no matter
how long it takes you
to open it again.

Whatever the Path

There is no single path to God;
every way can be the right one if
you follow it with the right mind.

So don't judge others for theirs,
or think you should join them;
not everyone can or should follow

the same path. Stay on yours
until you find that following it
in the right way makes it right,

whatever the path.

Love Is More Important

> If you want to know how to follow God,
> remember that love is more important
> than deeds, however good they might be.
>
> Remind yourself of this whenever you
> are tempted to imagine that someone
> else's way is better than yours;
>
> it might be, for them, but your journey
> is to follow God in your own way,
> whatever that is, and in all things.
>
> The rest will take care of itself,
> which is the only rest you'll ever find,
> and the only rest you finally need.

Letting Go of Getting It Right

Some teachings are difficult to grasp;
others are as close to you as your breath.
Here's one of those: as long as God is
content, you, too, should be content.

And God is content, not worrying
about the external things in your life—
what you should wear, or eat, or say.
So why should you?

Let go of your need to get it right,
Remember that you are responsible
for what you do, but what matters
is that God takes form in you.

You Are the Gift

Why am I so weak? you wonder. I tell you this:
your weakness is one way God reminds you that
your strengths keep you from seeing who you are;
for the weaknesses in your life are one of the ways
God desires to liberate you; when you finally rest in
God's enough-ness and embrace being in yourself,
a pure nothingness in the face of God's all-ness,
you will see that you are the gift God desires.

Free Yourself of Your Self

It is often true that the simplest teachings
are the most difficult to accept, and this
is one of them: You must learn to free
yourself of your self, with all your gifts.
This may seem untenable to you, but
the truth is that only by relinquishing
your hold on what you think is yours—
not once, but again and again—will you
find the inner freedom you long for.

Always in All Ways

So you wish to begin a new life?
Then begin here and now with
whatever you are doing, however
dark and meaningless it may seem.

For your work is to find God
always and in all ways—
at all times, in all places, in any
company, and in all ways.

This is the wayless way that
leads us to grow in everything
and increase unceasingly,
without end.

Serenity and Service

Some think it best to withdraw from the busy world
and find an inner peace that is without distraction,
but I say this: Whatever serenity you find within
your soul should open you to serve others in their need.
This is the wisdom of the wayless way that will lead you
to see that inner and outer, serenity and service, are not
two but finally one. Don't think this, but practice it
here and now; the rest will follow.

Part Two

EMBRACING
DARKNESS

Where Did You Come From?

Some think this must have been a lofty place,
something as radiant as the face of God.

But I disagree. It would be better to seek
the eternal abyss of divine being, that still

desert where God simply is in a silence
and darkness beyond knowing, desiring,

and possessing. There, in that darkness,
is where you first emerged; there, you'll

become so poor that you'll be free of all
the knowledge you have within yourself—

as you were at the beginning when there
was nothing but God within you, and what

you were was yourself—and nothing else.

In That Darkness

If you desire to find God, look beyond all
that is within your soul; gaze into the still
desert where God dwells, and ever has

since before you were, and ever will,
even beyond your death. In that darkness,
which might seem like death itself,

God cannot be prevented from loving
you, since doing so would mean that
God would cease to be God—indeed,

this would kill God, if that is imaginable;
and since it is not, know that nothing
can deter God from loving you, not

your unbelief or your worst failings
or anything you have failed to do, even
if all this seems unforgivable to you.

It Is Complicated

It is impossible
to find your well-being
in the external world
when the source of
your being is inside
of you.

It is just that simple.
And living justly
and loving fully
outside is just
that demanding.

If You Are Suffering

If you are suffering
or sad, it is because
you turned
to the world
with your heart
and love to give
what is
only God's
to contain.
So why are you
surprised that
in turning to
the world
you found
despair?

Bad Things and Good People

Those bad things
that come
to good and bad people
alike have nothing
to do with God
who creates, sparks, and
encourages nothing
of bitterness
or despair or pain.

Giving Your Life for Justice

You can give your life for justice
as so many saints before you have done,
and be without the pain and worry
those have who do not know or
love the Holy One whose joy
is in justice for the world—
and not in worldly things.

God Who Comforts

Blessed be God, who comforts us
when losses come, St. Paul says.
What do we have to lose?
Possessions, friends, and well-being.
There is an art in suffering well
in consolation and remembering,
and becoming aware
of the same
in ourselves.

Goodness Cannot Be Born

Goodness cannot be born,
but repeats itself again
and again by germinating
what is good.
There is a oneness
to the good, and to be,
do, speak, hear, and touch
goodness is to be
with the all-good God,
and to be in God.

You Must Free Yourself of Your Self

Do you desire wisdom? Then why look
outside yourself? Turn to God who is
a light shining and burning within you,
no matter how thick the darkness might
seem to you. But you must free yourself
of your self, and the more you do this,
the more light will pour into your life.

So don't strive to seek this outside
yourself; strive rather to free your
self in the ground of your soul,
and wait for the new birth that
will happen when God, who is
the true light, is born in you.

The Best Way of All

The best way is not a way that seeks to know,
but one that relinquishes this desire, along with
everything else; if you must seek something,

desire the blessedness that has neither a past
nor a future, and cannot become larger or
smaller. There, dwelling in the darkness of

an unknowing about how God is acting
within you, you'll come to delight in yourself
just as God delights in God's self—these

are not two things, but one. While it is good
to grasp this, it is far better to be grasped by it
and to experience it in freedom and peace.

What You Have That Is Good

What you have that is good
is what gives you pleasure
and becomes your joy.
But that is to see goodness
in your life as being
about you. It is not.
What is good is given
as the sun gives itself to
the vine and to the fruit.

There Is So Much We Need

O goodness
O truth
O justice,
there is so much
we need
and so few places
where we may lay
our heads.

Consider Your Suffering

Consider your suffering to be
like the merchant who,
for the sake of earning a profit,
will travel great distances
over dangerous roads,
with little sleep and
unhappy accommodations;
or like the knight who
risks his personal safety
and property for the sake
of uncertain honor that
will soon pass away;
how much more than these
will be the inheritance
you receive
from your hardships!

Child of God

Would you like to become
a child of God?
By struggle and will
you can only go so far.
But there is a higher power
in you that is not apart from you,
in the ground of your soul,
where, already, you are
one with God.

God Is Near

God is near
and without trouble,
suffering,
or pain.

Where are you
when you find
yourself
in trouble,
suffering,
or pain?

What it is
is pain, only
when we are God-
estranged.

Ask God to Free You of God

(i)

In the scriptures we read, *Blessed are the poor
in spirit, for theirs is the kingdom of heaven.*
What does this mean? I tell you it means this:
to desire nothing and know nothing and possess nothing.

Others imagine it means clinging to holy acts
and pious devotions, thinking that such things
will make us holy, but all this really means is
that they are asses on the inside who know nothing.

(ii)

I say this: as long as you try to carry out God's will,
you'll never become truly poor; first, you must let go
of your will as completely as you can, becoming
as free as you were before you were created.

Then ask God to free you of God; only then will you
grasp the truth that you are one with the highest angels
in your soul, desiring what you first were and becoming
what you first desired—in the single love which is God.

Much of Our Suffering

So much of our suffering
is in our illusions
of separation,
our distance,
and the ways
we allow unlikeness
with God to mask
our true identity.

God Is Always Within You

You sometimes imagine you are lost in darkness,
especially when you fail or face suffering in your life.

But I agree with an ancient teacher who reminds us
that God is the ground of your soul, like a spring

of living water; if someone were to throw dirt on it,
it becomes choked and blocked so that you lose

sight of it, but if you remove the dirt, you'll find
that spring again, whole and unblemished as it always is.

The presence of that living water is not your work,
for it is always living, but it is your task to keep it clear.

Nothing else matters.

Room Enough

We talk and talk and talk, and all
this brings us no closer to wisdom.

If you wish to understand the deep
truth that is in God and in yourself,

keep still and listen; become poor
in yourself, desiring nothing and

knowing nothing and possessing
nothing. Only when you are empty

of all your chatter will there be
room enough in you to receive

the gift of wisdom you long for.

One Love

Among the mysteries of love is this:
God has only one love, knowing no
bounds and flowing forth as Spirit—

and this gives shape and form to
God's wholeness in us and in all
that is. Including you.

This is the reason that I say
there is no Why in God, no need
to justify this love, which simply

is, ever seeking all who need it.
What would it mean if you also
lived like this, knowing no Why

to justify what you do or who
you are? What would this freedom
feel like for you?

Tend the Seed of God Within You

Know this: you have an outer and inner self,
and while you naturally serve the outer part—
worrying about what you should wear or eat, or
how you should live with others—the inner self
is what matters most and holds your nobility.

How can I explain this to you in a way you might
understand? Think of it this way: a pear tree's seed
will grow into a pear tree, just as a nut tree's seed
will become a nut tree, each becoming what it is.

So it is with you: the seed of God within you
grows into God; tend that seed, and do away
with the weeds that threaten to choke it out—
though even these cannot ever extinguish it.

For whether or not you see it, that seed will gleam
and glow, shining and burning in your life,
always seeking to become God in you.

Unholy Comfort

There's an ordinary comfort
in your losses, and though this
is not holy, consider this:
A person has a hundred coins
and then loses forty. To ponder
the lost forty is despair, and
to long for what was lost
is only to hallucinate.

What good does it do?
Turn your full attention
to those sixty coins left;
they are something, while
the others are nothing.

In days of pain
remember not to forget
the days of goodness.

This Changes Everything

(i)

Many people think that what has happened
is finished, just as they imagine that what is
in the future is fate; fair enough. But I say
that God is always creating, desiring to make
all things new—both those behind us, in the past,
and those that still lie before us in the future.

(ii)

Things aren't always what they seem to be.
If you stick a piece of wood in a pool of water,
it appears to your eyes that the wood is bent
where it enters the pool, but this is not so;
so, too, with God who is always creating
within you, in the past as in the future.

(iii)

When you look at things with your inner eye,
you'll find that God can change what is past
for you as well as what has not yet come to be;
knowing this is true in your life may startle you.
Even if you don't understand this, practice it
in your life until you do; this changes everything.

God Has Not Left You

Your pain does not mean
God has abandoned you,
but your comfort places do.
Where is your God? David hears
a voice taunting him because
he already knows the answer:
that his comfort has been his despair,
while the One who already knows
his pain is ever with him there.

Look Within Yourself for Truth

Some people think that Truth is something
they need to find; in this, they are both right
and wrong, because we must find Truth
again and again in our life. But know this:
Truth is not outside you, in some far-off way
of thinking or knowing; Truth is within you,
as close to you as your breath and as deep
as the deepest sea. Do you realize what this
means? If so, why do you waste your time
and energy looking outside of yourself?

Listen into the Wilderness

So you want to meet God and hear the eternal Word?
Desiring this will take you on a journey into the heart
of now, but to arrive, you must first let go of your self.

Abandon what you expect and hope for, and when
you've emptied yourself of this, you'll have room
for God to come to you, but not as you imagined.

Don't expect great fanfares or grand gestures. Listen
into the wilderness within; love yourself boldly, beyond
all that you've done well or failed to do. Begin today.

Listen to Seneca

Even Seneca knew how we are
to find comfort in suffering and pain.
Whatever has befallen you,
imagine that you prayed for this,
for you would have so prayed
had you only known that this
was God's will for you.

The Rest You Desire

(i)

At the heart of who you are is the ground
that is no ground, the place that is no place,
the endless source and boundless center where
God dwells—not in some manner or another,
but without any manner, in the naked and
divine nature which is the ground of
God's oneness—and yours.

(ii)

If you wish to rest in that oneness, and,
more than this: if you wish become one in
your life and discover the oneness of your life,
desire to enter that ground and dwell there;
when you do, you'll find you are one with
the One who is one with you in that ground
of oneness. Just as everything flows from this
oneness, so, too, does the rest you desire
in the innermost depths of your life.

You Don't Know

What you think you know,
you don't, really.
And what you do,
you don't really do—
if you are in God's will.
When you wish to know
nothing but God,
this is eternal life.
What else matters?

The Heart's Desire

Your heart's desire
will fill your mouth,
your actions, and your labor.
You will know what you
love by what you
say, where you go,
and what you do.
Your heart's desire
is easily revealed.

Who You Are

Who you are is much simpler
than any imagining or looking
or finding; who you are
you'll find in renouncing,
not receiving, in the joy
that comes when comfort
and happiness become
less important, and when
God alone *is*, in you,
that's God alone,
rejoicing.

Your Home

Of course it is dark where you stand
if this is far from the crowd, and even
from those you love, as well as your
memories, learning, and your will.
These all will spread you thin.
Whatever you might use to find yourself
is what sends you in many directions,
away from that noble birth of God in you.
This is why our Lord, at twelve, stayed
behind in the Temple in Jerusalem when
his beloved parents believed he needed
to go home—he was already there.
Who you are is not found out there,
somewhere, or anywhere else.

One of God's Consolations

For one who has lost much,
maybe a friend, a spouse,
or a child, perhaps a livelihood,
health, or anything precious,
there is a way God fills
the vacuum of that loss.

There is good reason
why you may feel closer
to the One after you
have lost another.

Light Shines in Darkness

Light shines in darkness,
John says, and Paul adds,
Virtue is perfected in weakness.
What is this but God's inscrutable justice
in which even the darkest of times
somehow come together
in the saving, blessing,
and comforting of those who
find themselves in trouble?

God's Promise

It is God's
promise that all
your pain will
one day be
turned into joy.

This may not
comfort you now,
but that is the
point of hard-to-
understand truth.

You Cannot Have Both

Which do you desire,
wine or water?
Because you cannot have
both in the same cask.
In fact, it is difficult
to enjoy wine from
a cask not entirely
free of its previous
liquid—which is why
pouring the water out
is necessary before you
should fill it with wine.
It's the same for you:
pour out what distracts
you, and make room
for the single love
that alone fulfills.

When in Darkness

When you are in darkness,
feeling pitiful or alone,
remember you are
blessed with a soul
that is more receptive
to the Spirit and
closer to love,
joy, and peace
than you were
when life seemed grand.
This is what
blessed are the
poor in spirit
means.

The Way to Consolation

Believe this, or
learn it some other way:
the consolation of God
can only come to
those who have
become poor and
empty of the world.
To them—call theirs
darkness if you wish—
there is joy and comfort.

So you want to find God?

Then seek to become one in your life.
Pay attention to what divides your heart—
your pride, your vanity, your selfishness.
As you remove these from yourself, you'll
find your way into the Oneness that is God,
which is always within you. So put aside
all that distracts you, and you'll find
true nobility and rest, blessedness
and contentment of heart. There,
you'll find the divine ground
within you; there, you'll become
wholly still, wholly one with the One.

Soul Arising

If it were possible
to empty a cup
completely, and
to keep it empty
of everything,
even air,
then that cup might
lose all properties
of cupness, and
float on up to the sky.

So your soul rises
when it becomes so
empty as to lose
itself in God.

Remember Your Source

> Every creature,
> like water to a river,
> flows and returns
> to its source because
> of the fervent love
> that draws and leads
> it to the One.

The Spark and the Fire

> When a physical fire
> is kindled in wood,
> a single spark holds
> all the fire's fullness
> and communicates with
> all that brings it to flame.
> The father of the spark
> is the fire and the mother
> of the spark that wood,
> and in this manner
> is your soul begotten
> of the One.

Gratitude

To have much
is to have much
to lose; we ought
to remember this
when we face a loss,
so that this might
become our place
to be thankful.

My Loss

There are times when my feelings
of loss are out of proportion to what is
real and true. For instance, a friend once
lent me three coats for chilly weather—
but then he took one of them back.
The fullness of my gain was but for a time,
while my loss only reminded me that all
things come to us on loan.

Like a Stone

Loving God and willing the good
may one day become so natural
to you that you are like a stone
that will fall to the ground no matter
how long it sits on a ledge high above
the earth, even for a thousand years,
so that once it begins to move,
that stone can do
no other than
fall
to the
ground.

When You Are Bereft

To love God sufficiently
is to be one of
God's very children,
and to hear words
such as those spoken
by God the Father
to God the Son:
You are my beloved,
you please me.

This is the progeny
of a poor spirit,
of those with
nothing of their own,
who are naked
before God.

Little by Little

Among the many things I've taught, one
stands above the others: God gives to all

things equally, no matter how small and
insignificant we might think them to be,

and as these things flow forth from God,
as we also do, they are equal and alike.

This is true for women as for men, for
the angels as for all the creatures who are

in this world. Remember this, and consider
things as they were when they first came

from God—as you also once did—and
little by little you'll learn to love them

with the same love that God does and
find that they are in God and are God.

Begotten Is Begetting

God created the world
in the eternal present,
such that everything
is still being created.
This is a continuous project.

There is neither then
nor when, but only
the boundless moment
of this eternal Now.
Even the Son of God
was begotten
in eternity
in this way
of begetting,
which has
no beginning
and is without end.

Nothing Else Matters

If only you could know how things
are in God, and how you are in God,

then you'd see that God contains them—
and you—completely and wholly.

God's one desire is that you seek
that wholeness and find it in God,

which is to say in your ground;
this is rest. Nothing else matters.

God Draws Us

There is a divine alluring
as the Holy One pulls each of us
toward the sacred heart, the place
where every creation finds itself
satisfied and transformed.
After all, God says, *I will
draw that soul and carry her
into the wilderness,
speaking to her heart.*

Nothing-More Prayer

Lord, I want nothing more than to be with You in this
divine moment, despite my body and in unity of soul,
and regardless of what suffering I now know,
I realize that everything I am is with You and in You
and all things are good that come together in this
holy unity and mystery. Amen.

A Body That Suffers

Perhaps a body that suffers
is like a precious piece
of silver or gold that is already
pure and beautiful, but is also
destined to become a goblet
at the highest table;
so it is soldered and smelted,
which is perhaps what the apostle
meant by saying it gives us joy
to be considered worthy
to suffer for the name.

Give Me Trouble

I will be with you
in all trouble,
God says, *and*
I will answer you
and rescue you.

In that case, let me say
with St. Bernard,
Lord, give me some trouble
now and always, and come
answer, rescue, and
remain here, please.

God-Friend

Everyone knows the comfort we feel
when, in pain or trouble, a friend
is near to listen—or, better, to sit
beside us and share our very distress.
Our suffering is then absorbed,
at least a bit, by another who cares.
How much more does our God, who
suffers with us and beside us,
comfort us in order to lessen the brunt
of this storm we are in.

Part Three

AWAKENING TO LIGHT

Where God's Radiance Dwells

Many people imagine that the sun and the stars
are the highest things that are, but I tell you that
the soul is higher than all this. So why reach beyond
what you always carry within you? Look within
and find there the highest heights of God—no matter
how low you might feel yourself to be. For God
is not only God for you, but always God within you,
and the greatest truth of God is the one you'll find
in your innermost depths where God's radiance dwells.

You Say That You Cannot See

You say that you cannot see where to go.
Well, this is darkness and also light.
Our God always creates in a flash.
Don't imagine that in creation God
went day by day. Moses tells it that way
because he thought we couldn't understand:
God willed, spoke, and things were!

You see, God works without means
and images, and the less you rely
on what you see, the more receptive
you will be to God's inward working.

Awakening to Light

When Paul fell to the ground, hit by a light from heaven,
the scriptures say that he got up, opened his eyes, and
    saw nothing.

At that moment, the apostle's eyes were opened by
    that light
and that fall and he began to see all things as nothing.

Only when he rose from the ground, blinded,
was he finally able to see God. As the Song says,

I sought him whom my soul loves; I sought him,
but he gave no answer.

The Light of God

Every night there is, or ever was, was not without light,
but the light was veiled; sun shines in the nighttime,
but its light is hidden from us. Still, as the sun eclipses all
other light in this solar system, so does the light of God,
even when hidden, shine more brightly than all else.
So if you seek answers in the darkness, remember that
the true source of all light and dark is always present.

You Will Have It

You may think to yourself,
These are such fantastic things you describe,
Eckhart, but I can't perceive them.
I understand; it's like that for me, too.
But rest assured that this state of being,
with God alive in you, is both noble and common—
common in a way that can never be purchased,
at any price. If your intentions are pure, and
your will untethered, you will have it.

Clear Water

What is dense and muddy here
is clear and clean there, in God.
Imagine that you were to pour clear water
into a clean basin and, still as still can be,
look into that water down to the bottom.
Its shining clarity, and absence of opacity,
would be evident from above to below.
It is just so with human beings who stand
free, unified in themselves,
with God so clear.

The Power of Practice

> To live a life grounded in God,
> you don't need information;
> you need to be informed by
> the spark of divine presence
> you always carry within you.
> But you'll have to practice
> this, with concentration,
> like you would if you were
> learning a skill or an art.

Christmas Is Today and Every Day

At the heart of everything is one love;
the love that gave birth to all of creation
is the same love that was born on that
first Christmas morning, in Bethlehem,
the light that shone in the darkness.

That same love is the light being born
in you each day, without ceasing.

So, open yourself to this light, and
celebrate the coming of God into
this world in your darkness—for
Christmas is not long ago and far away,
but here and now, today and every day.

Breaking-Through to Become Free of God

One of the great teachers has said that breaking-
through is better than flowing-forth, and I agree,
because in flowing-forth I know myself as I am
in God, as a creature among other creatures.

But when I break-through all this, and become
free of my own will to know and even to be,
I come to what is far greater than this, becoming
free of God's works—and, finally, free of God;

there, I receive an impulse that raises me above
all that is, including the highest angels; there, I
have such great wealth that nothing, not even God,
can satisfy me, because in breaking-through

I become one with God and know myself as
an immovable cause that causes everything.
Don't seek to understand this but to live it,
and when you do, you'll begin to understand.

You Will Not See

You will not see what is hidden,
even when it comes in the form of a word.
At night, in silence, a hidden word was spoken
to me like a thief at night, a wise man once said.
O this whispering stillness, this quiet revelation!
We yearn for this, but you will never see it
even though it is shining in the dark.
What brings light to your understanding
may never be grasped or perceived
in the way you are accustomed to seeing.
This is both darkness and light.

A Saving Equation

If you wish to be blessed, you will not
find this through what you do, no matter
how good all of that might be;

instead of this, empty yourself of doing
and knowing, and open yourself to receive
what you cannot know or do alone,

for in this matter, you'll receive far more
than you could ever give. And know this:
the unendingness of your receiving is

identical with God's unending desire
to give; only then can you know with God's
knowledge, and love with God's love.

Little by Little

(i)

Day after day you worry about how you should
live your life, what you should do, and why.
Little by little this burdens you and you become
an anxious manager of your uncontrollable life;
staying on this path, year by year, you accumulate
mountains of anxiety and oceans of distress.

(ii)

What I say to you is simple, though it may
be hard to grasp: Let go of all this! Free yourself
of your self! This is difficult at first, but practice
relinquishing one worry at a time, and see
what happens; to help you, remember that God
gave you your soul as a pure and precious gift.

(iii)

As you learn to let go of your worries, trust
that you are finding your way back into the deep
goodness of God, for this is the radiance your life
depends on. And remember: God is an unspoken
word within you; knowing this is everything.
Nothing else matters.

You Are the Cause of God

Many think that loving God is
the highest thing we can do,
but I disagree.
I tell you that you
must free yourself of God for
God's sake, for your true self
is one with the God beyond God—
and is the ground of all that is,
including you.
There, in that self
which is unborn and never dies,
you'll come to know that your
very existence is because of God—
and for this reason, you'll see
that you are the cause of all things,
even of God.
That may sound
outrageous, but it's true, and while
you must not understand this,
doing so will help you break-
through to the eternal Now
in your life, which is freedom.

Free Yourself

You've often heard me say that it is best
to seek detachment, which is to say:
free yourself of your self and of all things
outside of you. But remember that
this is not something to accomplish;
it is about relinquishing, about letting go
of your desire to have something, or
to become someone. Try finding your
self in your nothingness, in the not-
being beyond having and doing.

If you are wondering how to do this,
I'd put it this way: Let go of your self
as much as you can, and then some more;
then open your self to be in-formed back
into the simple goodness of the one love
which is God; there, you'll be one with
the One who is the ground within you.

Heaven Is Cheap

Some think that Heaven is an illusion;
others, that it is an unattainable place.
I say something quite different:
Heaven is cheap, because it is on sale
to everyone at the price they can afford.
So the real question is not whether
Heaven exists, but whether you are
willing to give up the one thing needful
to attain it: your self-will that makes you
think you're in charge of everything,
even Heaven.

Three Ways in God

We all live within the circle of eternity,
and in this circle are three ways that lead
us in God and ground us in our true self.

The first calls us to seek God in all that is,
by every way, with many diverse actions
by which love burns deep within us.

The second is a wayless way, raising
us up above ourselves and all things,
but here we fail to see God as God is.

The third is the way of being-at-home,
seeing God who is the still desert, beyond
images, transcending what words can do.

This is a miracle! How astonishing to be
both outside ourselves and within, to grasp
and to be grasped, to hold and to be held.

Our deepest desire is to live like this,
ever dwelling in peace in the eternal Now,
circling through and beyond every way.

Your Somethingness in God

This is a simple but amazing truth: something and
nothing are not the same. What is nothing cannot receive
something from something; you are nothing in yourself,
but in God you are something, and that somethingness
is perfect—in and through the nothingness that is God.

So why stay sheltered in your little something-self, full
of fear and anxiety? Why not forget yourself in your no-
thing-ness, and open yourself to knowing that God's ground
and your ground are one? What more is there to
desire or know than some measure of this allness?

Peace Is Not Your Goal

As far as you are in God,
to that extent you live in peace;
as far as you are not in God,
to that extent you lack peace.

But it follows from this that
peace is not a goal you can
directly attain; what else is
there to do than to concentrate
all you are on living in God?

Practice this, and when you do
you will find your way to peace
and know peace as your way.

Do Not Seek the Way

(i)

Some people want to savor God in one way
and not another, seeking to possess God
through the use of one devotion rather than
another. This might seem right at first, but
I say that it is quite wrong, for if we are
to take God rightly, then we must do so in
all things—in tribulation and in thriving,
in tears and joy, in all the ways that are.

(ii)

If you believe that you lack true devotion
and even the intent to be faithful, and think
that you lack God for this reason, and if
you grieve over this, your sorrow becomes
your true devotion and real intention; it is
best not to seek God in any particular way,
for when you do, you might find that way,
but you'll surely lose the God who is not to be
found in any one way. Seek God, then, on
the wayless way where God will find you.

Darkness Will Do

The mystery of your life
is that you are to do

nothing less than this:
to radiate God. Don't

look for light outside
yourself; look inside;

darkness will do as
the place to start.

Filling What Is Empty

God is no carpenter who, seeing an empty wall
or cleared space for a building, works at a leisurely
pace, starting and stopping, even leaving such
a project unfinished. God is always at work,
filling what is empty and bare with God's self,
overflowing into you like what happens when
the clouds finally clear and the sun simply must
burst out into the pure and endless blue of the sky.

No Matter What

No matter what happens, and whatever suffering
or adversity comes to you, remember this truth:
You still retain the image of God, for the light
of God remains ever radiant within you.
For the scripture written by St. John
is true of you when he wrote that
the true light shines in the darkness.
Because this is true, even if you do not
see it, embrace the light that shines
within you, regardless of what you see
and no matter how deep the darkness you face.

Why worry about growing old?

In truth, you are as young as your soul,
which is as young as it was on the day
God first made it. That's true enough,
but there's more: your soul is younger now
than it was when God made it.
What this means is not beyond me,
though I can't explain it better than this.
You'll understand it only when you stop
your worrying and start living into
the youthfulness that is your soul.

Pouring In

God's way of filling our emptiness may be
compared to the would-be child in nascent form
in its mother's womb: the moment such substance
is present, there is God pouring in God's own self,
a living soul, to fill that imperceptible body.
This is what the Lord meant by saying,
Listen! I am standing at the door, knocking;
if you hear my voice, and open the door,
I will come in.

Heaven Refuses to Keep a Distance

Some imagine that Heaven is immense,
an idea that might seem to make sense.

But Heaven refuses to keep a distance
from all that has fled from it and taken up

the lowest place of all, which is the fate
of the earth and all within it—even you.

Because of this, Heaven renounced its
vastness and gave itself entirely to the earth

to make it fertile. And you dare to think
you're not part of this astonishing gift—

the spark in you that desires God alone,
which is the true source of your one hope?

The Rest You Desire

Most of the time, you live your life distracted
and worried by many things, and when you do
you look away from your deepest identity, which
is ever at rest in the oneness of God's ground.

To transcend this downward spiral, train
your inner eye on that oneness, which is love—
which is God's ground in you, which is your
inner self, which is God-in-and-through-you.

For in this is the rest you desire in your rest-
lessness, and as you live into this you'll find
that your ground and God's ground are one
in the single love that is God in and through you.

Always Be Ready for the Miracle

Don't ask for anything less than this:
that God might be with you. If you
feel that you do not or cannot have
this grace, do you at least desire it?
And if you can't even desire it, then
try desiring to desire it, for even this
is pleasing to God. So, start here, and
always be ready for the miracle.

More God than I Am Myself

(i)

A great teacher, St. Augustine, tells us
that *through love we become what we love,*

and wonders if it is also true, then, that
if we love God, do we become God?

I tell you that this is so, since when I
love I am more God than I am myself.

(ii)

Love God and let the rest flow from this,
and in that flow you'll come to know that

you should respect and consider all others
as yourself; when you come to grasp this,

you'll begin to know that whatever
happens to someone else, whether good

or bad, is happening to you as well.
What would that mean for you today?

Your True Beauty

I've said this many times and in many ways:
you must die in order to live. You must live
so that your whole life is love, and let go of
all that you are, relinquishing everything,
for only then can you ever hope to discover
your true self.

This confuses the fearful, worries the proud,
and offends the powerful, and you'll only
begin to grasp it when you let go of all you
think you are and all you hope to become;
abandon your false self and cast yourself out
into the fathomless depths of the Godhead—
beyond every image and thought you might
have of God, for only there will you find
the beauty within you which reflects
the god-ness of God.

God Sees No Sin

Some teachings are clear to our minds;
others are difficult, not in themselves

but because of the mystery they contain
within themselves. One of these is this:

God knows only God, and sees every-
thing as it is within God's own self,

and in this seeing, God sees no sin—
not yours, not anyone's.

So why, in your pride, do you continue
to see yourself in your sin, or others in theirs?

For this turns you from God's way of seeing
and being, which holds you and others

and all that is becoming in the oneness of love.

The One Needful Thing

If you want to know whether what
you are doing builds God's kingdom,
ask yourself this: Do my actions hurt
others? Do they trouble my heart?
Do they make me feel better than others?
If so, you're like Martha who concerned
herself with many things, while missing
the one needful thing. *What is that one
thing?* you wonder. You'll not ask this
when you're truly at peace in your life;
you'll simply know.

There God Shines

Knowledge is great, but desire is greater,
because it leans into what it does not know.

But God is beyond all that knowledge can
grasp or desire can want; where knowing

and desiring end, there is darkness and there
God shines—within you and in all that is.

Becoming a New Creation

Imagine this if you can:
when God performs a work
of grace, like turning you
toward what is good—
which God is doing all
the time—this is greater
than if God were to make
a new world. Imagine this:
such a turning is greater
than calling light from
darkness, or bringing
form out of chaos. When
you experience yourself
turning to what is good,
you'll know this is also
happening in you.

What About You?

At the heart of all that is, there is one love
in one God; all that God works in creatures
and in God's own divinity derives from this
oneness, and on account of this, God is God.

What about you? The glory of your soul
lies in this oneness and not in all that you
might still do or fail to do; practice dwelling
in God's love; the rest will follow.

When you do, you'll come to see that
you, in your nothingness, are everything,
for God pours into your emptiness all
that is noblest and purest and highest.

God Delights in You as God

In all my teaching, there is one truth
I've never yet said, and it is this: God delights
in God's self. And this truth belongs to it:
God delights in us with that same delight.
But there's more:
God delights in us not as creatures,
but rather delights in us as creatures
who are God. This sounds outrageous,
I know, and it is—and in this outrage
lies the heart of joy.

To Love as God Loves

When people ask me what they should do,
I tell them this: Love others as much as
you love yourself. If you find
that you don't love some people as
much as you love yourself, then this
is because you've not yet learned
to love yourself fully.
For what you do not love in others
you've not yet learned to love in yourself;
work on this and you'll begin to discover
what it means to love as God loves.

Make the Best of Everything

Some commands are a duty; others, a gift.
One of the latter is this:
Make the best of everything.
Which is to say, expect to receive
God in everything, for God is
already in everything,
even in you—above all
where you least expect it.
So I'll say it again:
Make the best of everything.
And by this I mean: in wealth and
poverty, darkness and light,
sickness and health.
You'll only find peace if you
make the best of everything.

Learn to Rest

What is the difference
between you and God?
God never rests, but is
always creating through
the one love that God is—
and part of that work
is God's desire that you
should be consumed
in God, dissolved in God,
and wholly transformed
into love. Which is God.

You'll come to know
this as you learn to rest
in God, turning from
everything
and living as God does—
in simplicity and
nakedness and
joy.

Obedience Isn't What You Think

So you want freedom?
Then give up insisting
you know what you need.

Because you don't, since
desire limits you to what you
imagined and hoped for.

Freedom begins when
you let go of that hope,
renouncing your will for

this or that in your life,
which is obedience.
Which is freedom.

What Is the Hardest Thing of All?

Be ready to be surprised: it is to love yourself
as you are, not as how you see yourself or hope

to be seen by others. You'll know you're on
the right path when you find that you love

everyone as much as you love yourself. How
will you know this is true? You'll love them

for who they are, as bearers of God, ignoring
what you might want them to be—or become.

It's as simple as this and as demanding, and
you have a lifetime to practice getting it right.

Breaking-Through

Of all the miracles within our reach,
this is one of the greatest: God becomes God
when all creatures speak God forth;
in that speaking, God is born.
To do this is religion.

But the highest thing, beyond this,
is even more audacious: to break-through
to the Godhead, which is the ground, depth,
flood, and source from which we all came.

When I enter this ground, rooting myself in this depth,
giving myself to this flood and honoring this source,
I find no one has missed me; there I un-self myself,
and there God un-becomes what I first imagined.

This is a deep mystery; you will understand
this in poverty and exile or not at all.
I wish you well with the journey.

What Is a Free Mind?

It's not what you think.
Because it's not about
thinking. It's about
the state of mind
you find when
you let go of the need
to get it right, and
abandon the self you
thought you were.
What's left is freedom,
untroubled and
unfettered by anything,
but you'll only find it
when you go out of
what is your own
and refuse to seek
your own interest
in anything at all,
even in yourself.

Looking in All the Wrong Places

If you set out looking for something,
whatever that might be, you won't find it.
What's worse, you'll miss finding every-
thing else that was always there for you.

You Are the Gift

Don't worry about doing the right thing.
No matter what you do or how hard
you try, you'll always fail.
Focus instead on who you truly are,
which won't be helped with striving.
Stop worrying about your worth,
and turn from seeking peace in things
outside of you, however good they are.
Accept yourself as you are, and you'll
begin to know that you are the gift you
do not deserve and could never earn.

Everything Is God

So, you want to know God?
It's not what you think;
abandon what you thought
God was or needed to be,

and when you've let go of
that God, you might be ready
to receive God as God is, in
the abyss of God's God-ness.

Be ready to be surprised
to find that you are God's only-
begotten and you are finally
nothing less than . . . God.

It's Not About You

People often ask me
what they should do
to be faithful.
My answer is
always the same:
Let God be great
and strive to live
into that greatness,
because this is true
no matter how small
you think you are.

The Waking Heart

We read in the Book of Love, *I sleep,*
but my heart is awake. What can this mean?
The masters say this: If you were asleep
and could remain so for a hundred years,
and knew nothing of creaturely things
or of time, then you might come to know
what God is doing within you.

Let me ask you this: Do you sleep by day
or at night? If at night, then why do you
fear the dark, which is where you will
come to know what Love longs to teach
you in your heart, which keeps watch?

Everything Will Become God

Some people think that finding God
depends on being in the right place,

praying in the right way, or keeping
company with the right people.

But I say this: strive to be in the right
state of mind, and you'll find God

finding you—no matter where you are
or how you pray or whom you're with.

If you do this, you'll see that everything
will become God for you. Everything.

Everything and Everywhere

So, you want
to find God?
Stop looking
for the right
place or time,
since God is
in everything
that is, and every-
thing is in God.
Try keeping God
present in your
mind and in your
striving and in
your loving,
and when you
do, you'll find
God always
and every-
where.

The Spark Within You

Each day you should do good toward others
without asking why or wondering what you might
gain for it; doing this is the reason you're here.

How should you do this? Not by focusing
your energies on yourself, or attending to
what is outside of you, but by setting aside

your self entirely and resting in the One
"I" who is always radiant within you. Enter
your innermost depths, into what I call

your ground, and there, in the midst of
all that might seem a darkness in your life,
you'll find the spark within you that no-

thing can overcome. Let all that you do
arise from that source, and you'll find that
everything will become radiant for you.

Tasting God in Everything

Some people complain that God is boring—
same old thoughts, exhausted from the start.

But I tell you that such a view is entirely
wrong, because the living God can't even

be expressed in your thinking, however
clever that might be. If you settle for such

a God, expect that when your thoughts
finally end, you'll lose that God entirely.

Faith begins when you learn to turn from
the God you've only thought about and

open yourself to the radiance that shines
in the dark; when you do this, you'll begin

to taste God in everything and everyone,
always and everywhere and in all ways.

The Rest Will Follow

We often worry
about where God is,
while all the while
God is wondering
where we are.

So where are you?
Don't worry about
the destination;
after all, your journey
is on a wayless way.

Concentrate on that,
and don't concern
yourself with where
you should go or
what you should do.

Choose to live
so that your whole life
becomes love; when
you do, the rest
will follow.

There Is Only One Birth

One of the great mysteries in life is this:
that there is only one birth in time, and
this birth takes place not in some dimly
imagined beginning, beyond us, but in
the true essence and inner ground of
the soul—yours and mine. But pay
close attention to this: this birth must
occur within you, and not only once;
your work is to wait to be born within it.

This birth is a promise as much for you
when you sin as for you when you are
good, and it even holds for those who
find themselves in Hell itself. Yes,
even for them, for their need is great,
and this lures the light which seeks
us in our deepest darkness. This is
the way of goodness, which is God,
pouring itself forth wherever needed—
and because it is everywhere, you can
be sure that it is within you, above all
in the heart of your darkness. So, quit
your worrying and get ready to be born—
again and again and again.

A Matter of the Heart

Don't look for the right words
or thoughts or ways to pray,
for you won't find God
by learning the right words
or cultivating the right kind
of devotion or pious practice,
for God is a matter of the heart.

The Hardest Truth

I've said this many times, because it's hard
to grasp, so bear with me as I say it again:
you must forsake God for God's sake in order
to die into life—nothing less than this will do.

This death is what God calls you to—not
the God of your thinking, which only exists
in your mind, but the living God; the greatest
honor you can pay God is to take leave of
God for God's sake. Free yourself of all
that you imagined God to be; only so can
you come to live into your nothingness.

There, you'll find God's true goodness,
and when you live like this you'll find that
the whole of your life will become love.

Part Four

LIVING IN RADIANCE

You Carry an Inner Radiance

A great teacher once said that if we think
of God as a word, then God is spoken;

but if God is a word unspoken, then God
is beyond speaking and knowing, beyond

words—but not beyond you, since you
carry an inner radiance which also is

beyond speaking and knowing, but not
beyond you in the nobility of who you

are in your soul; there, in that spark,
the unspoken God becomes radiant.

Learn to Break-Through Things

Finding God is like learning to write:
if you truly want to acquire this skill,
you've got to practice long and hard
at it, even when it seems difficult,

if not impossible; you have to begin
by learning how to form each letter,
committing it to memory until you
no longer need to concentrate on it.

It's the same with God: learn to break-
through things to the point that you
find God's radiance within them all,
even in the dark abyss of silence.

Restlessness and Radiance

We live our lives in restlessness and confusion
while always carrying a light within us that

no darkness can extinguish, and a love that
is stronger than every sort of hate, and when

you find that solitude in the inner motion
of your spirit—and not just in thinking

about God—you'll find that God will never
leave you and will shine forth in everything

and be radiant in all that is, even in you.

There Is No Death

You are two people. We all are.
There is in each of us an inner
and an outer person.
The outer is the old,
unconverted, coarse,
and growing older.
The inner is the new,
ever turning toward
the divine, ever younger.
There is no death for that
heavenly inner person
in whom God shines.

Savoring God

Have you ever wondered
why you love God as you do?
Is it for reasons of faith or eternity,
or by something that may come
to you as a return? No, the lover
of God savors all other things
for the sake of God, knowing
that God is everything and in all,
the ground of life in this world,
the One in me—and you.

You Are a Desert

You are a desert, so lay claim
to nothing, including yourself,
and allow this mystery to be
everything in your life.

This is mystery's birth in you,
and mystery's life through you.
You, too, are but a voice of one
crying in the wilderness, so do:
allow this voice of mystery
to cry out in you.

You Are a Construction Zone

Yes, you, here and now in this one
wild and precious life of yours,
you are always becoming new,
for God is in all that is, always
making all things new—even you.

To experience this, stop thinking
about outward things in your life,
which worry or confuse you,
and turn to that innermost part of
your soul, with all its radiance,
for it is there that God is ever
creating within you.
Only when you believe this
will you find it, and only when
you find this will you believe.

Don't Do Too Much

All those pieties and practices will help you,
and are most necessary, when God's Spirit
is not working in your inner person.
At such times, be sure to pray and sing
and study and fast. Go on pilgrimages.
And hope that when you make yourself
close to God, God will choose to return
to acting again in your soul. But when you
know God as present in your inner life,
you can let those disciplines fall away.
Then, you'll not be able to bear
spending so much time on
outward things.

Ridiculous Joy

If you've ever seen a horse running
gayly about in a wide-open meadow,
you'll know how God feels in finding
that everything in this life is equal and
alike in being what it is. And remember:
this includes you, even on your worst
of days; when God gazes upon you,
even then, imagine that crazy horse
bucking wildly and galloping all
about with bursts of ridiculous joy.

Virtue Shines Out, Day and Night

We come to the light in many ways.
One is to seek it in the dark and wait
for it to surprise us as it comes; another
is more certain: when you act virtuously
and offer yourself with generosity to others,
the inner life of your actions is a radiance
that shines out, day and night, and if
you listen quietly, you'll hear how
such generosity praises God and
sings a new song within you.

Everything Is One in God

God gives God's self to everything
equally; a fly, as it exists in God, is
nobler than the highest angel.

Don't be surprised when I tell you
that this is true for you as well:
your life, as it flows from God,

is one with that fly—and you,
too, are nobler than those angels,
and everything is one in God.

You and God

Why did God become human?
So that you might become God.
When Our Lord ascended into heaven,
he went beyond all created light,
beyond our ability to see or understand.

You may go there if you are dead,
meaning without self or likeness,
a one-of-a-kind, like God;
this is the pure unity
in which God made us,
the source we come from
and toward which we journey.

Asleep to Things

To comprehend the true practice of *Thy will be done*,
you have to imagine having no will at all,
joining yourself with the one holy will of God.

What if you were to fall asleep and remain so
for a hundred years, and then, when you woke,
you had no knowledge of things or of times past
or future plans? Only then would you understand
and see how to be without any will but God's.
As the scripture says, *I slept, but my heart was awake.*

Crying in the Wilderness

Remember that the first voice of grace
was that of the Baptist crying in the wilderness:
Prepare ye the way of the Lord.
How else to do that but by removing
everything that lies in the way?
There is a poverty of spirit
that ceases all seeking,
with a stripped-nakedness of being.
This alone is the way of freedom.

A Thousand Times More

Do not imagine for a moment
that your reason will ever
carry you to God.
Your natural light
extends only so far,
until fading into darkness.
There, in the dark beyond
your natural light, is where
God's holy radiance illuminates
everything beyond your imagining—
a thousand times more brightly.

When You Have Nothing

When you have nothing,
you have everything.
God has filled the poor
with good things,
and the rich have
been sent away
completely empty.
When you are poor,
you have lost much—
you are in pain
and discomfort,
in suffering and grief,
but now you have
the way, the truth,
and the life.

Open Your Self to the Radiance

So, you wish to know God? Look deep within
for the little spark that ever burns in your soul;
refuse what is outside of you, and open your self
to the radiance of that inner spark.

Focus all your attention on that little spark,
which will be satisfied with nothing but God
and refuses simply to learn about God; if this
is startling to you, how much more astonishing
it is to realize that the radiant light within you
won't be satisfied with what God is toward you.

That inner light insists on knowing where God
comes from. Where is that? Look into the depths,
all the way to the simple ground, the still desert,
where all you think about God counts as nothing
and where everything is finally nothing but God.

Light Is for the Humble

In Thy light we shall see light, sang David in the fields,
and the light of Thy face is impressed on me.
But then there is what we hear through Moses:
No one can see God and live.
What is the light for, but to remind
us of the darkness?
Light is only for the humble.

Stop Your Seeking

Pilgrimages are not necessary.
You may stop looking here and there.
Calling and pleading, as if from afar,
no more of this, too. The Lord
simply waits for an opening in you,
wanting and longing for you
a thousand times more than you
ever wanted in all of that
seeking and calling.

I Can't Feel God

How can I believe that God is there,
ready to fill my willing emptiness?
I can't feel God. Realize, then,
that your awareness of God is
from God, not from your own powers.
There will be times of God-concealment
and times of God-revealment; Christ said
as much to his friend Nicodemus:
The wind blows where it chooses, and you hear
the sound of it, but you do not know where it comes
from or where it goes. So it is with everyone who
is born of the Spirit.

When You Are Empty

When you are empty,
feeling bereft,
or not feeling much at all,
hesitate before trying
to fix your situation,
because this happens
to be just what
you are: a vessel
awaiting the fill
of heavenly
fullness beyond any
this-worldly feeling.

This Birth of God in Me

You ask: *This birth of God in me,*
how may I know it has taken place?
May I have a sign? Absolutely.
God in you now means that
nothing on earth can turn
your attention from the Holy One.
You'll become like the thousand leaves
on a tree struck by lightning
as they turn upwards,
every one facing
that fiery, startling light.
You'll have been turned around.

Breaking-Through Things

God is in everything that is, shining
forth with a radiance that enlightens
every darkness, but to see this you
must first break-through things and
allow God to take form within you.

How do you do this? Let go of your
desire to make it happen, and seek
that still desert where you'll find
that everything is in God and every-
thing, including you, is God.

Prayer for the Birth of God

May God be born in me
so dearly and truly
that God is all
that matters.
Then, all things
will become
God to me.
As a person
who stands looking
at the sun may turn aside
but still see
only the sun
in her eyes,
so may I see
only God
in what I see,
since God is being
born in me.

Fishhook-Love

Better than penance is love,
but to be true, your love of God
best be like a hook in a fish:
when the fisherman snags that fish,
and the hook is firmly set,
there is no creaturely getting away.
No matter how heavy the catch,
or how far down it may dive,
that fish is soon to see the face
of one who loves it back, and
the person with fishhook-love
for God belongs completely
to God.

To Meet God Alone

Can you meet God alone,
leaving behind everything
you may see in front of you?
There is a spiritual vision
to animate your imagination.
It is supernatural, and it is yours,
infused by love when it is love
alone that allows you to see.
This vision is an ecstasy
of love.

You Really Are

Who you really are
is where truth dwells,
solely and wholly filling
your inner parts where
the world cannot reach.

God arises in you there.

There, the voice of God,
and only that holy sound,
can be heard.

Identity Crisis

The next time you feel you don't know
who you are, remember that Jesus cleared
the temple of the moneychangers;
that temple is a metaphor for your soul,
and your soul is made like nothing else
on earth or in heaven, and God wants
that temple clear and empty,
to be alone there. So make room
for that aloneness, for this is who you are!

Clinging

The soul that continues
to cling to places, things, and
people, is withdrawing from God.
And the more that it clings,
feeling the world's comfort
and pleasure, the more wretched
it has become. There is good reason
why the apostle says that God
chooses the poor who are rich
in faith, because a poor soul
possesses what matters.

Clearing the Temple

Jesus clearing the temple,
sending out the merchants,
overturning the furniture,
setting all the doves to flight,
is our Lord preparing to speak
into our souls, where God
wants to get all
and entirely
alone with us.

You Will See Again

What do you see in the dark
and in the light, and what are
you trying so hard to see?

What we know and see
is what God has us know
and see. Illuminating is not
about brightness, but about
the One who illumines.

The apostle explains,
So you have pain now,
but I will see you again,
and your hearts will rejoice,
and no one will take
your joy from you.

And you will see again.

A Spark from the Fire

A roaring fire in the hearth
has many fiery sparks that come
from it, but when one leaves the log,
it is but a part sent up from
its flaming source;
that spark then seems
to forget itself,
straining upwards
in flight, soon
to be extinguished.
So the blessed
may be in the One,
hot and luminous,
able to burn and
hesitant to stray
too far.

Divine Fruit

In God alone the soul may rest.
St. Augustine said it:
Thou hast made us for thyself
and our hearts are restless
until they rest in thee.
For nothing better
than God is imaginable,
and God is the first
and the last and
the in-between,
just as God also is
the vine, the flowers,
and the fruit.

How Iron Puts on Fire

Let us then lay aside the works of darkness
and put on the armor of light, scripture says.
We have to put on Christ the way iron puts on fire.
Place a rod of iron into a furnace for ten minutes
and then pull it carefully back out again.
What is the iron now, but red hot and aflame—
like fire itself?

Beware of the Good People

Beware of the good people who say
you should be so perfect that neither joy
nor sorrow can move you. They are wrong.
There has never been a saint who was
without human feelings.

What makes a saint
is not the absence of emotion,
but not being moved from God
as a result of feelings—
either of joy or of woe.

Christ himself said, *I am
deeply grieved, even unto death*.
When your heart is wrung, keep
your soul sweetly grounded.

Whatever Happens

Whatever happens, know this,
that God began the work of you
by eyeing a perfect creature,
a noble person of being,
as sacred as the place
from which your soul came,
and holy as the place
where God would
be born in you.

God's idea of you
began before time,
and as the fire's heat
and its source
are dissimilar in nature
but much the same
in place and time,
so are you and God,
whatever happens,
close in most every way.

Love for Nothing

Would it not be amazing if we loved one another
in such a noble way that our love was without purpose
or reason, except to say that we love God for God's sake,
we love each other for each other's sake,
and we love goodness simply because it is good?
Loving one another would then be
loving for nothing more than love.

Make Me Less

I realized the other morning while praying
my Paternoster that when I said,
Thy kingdom come, thy will be done,
I was asking God to make me less
so that God might be more.
The more of me that falls away,
the more eternal bliss the newborn
in me will discover.

Stay Inside

When someone says,
Pray for me, I often think,
Why? Your true and noble source
is a blossoming Spirit
of the One and Holy God.
Stay inside. Do not leave
your very treasure; you
have it right there within you.
I pray, God be praised,
such blessedness.

How to Love This World

How to love this world
that so often wants
to hurt you
is the question.
We must love and
know each thing,
no matter how big
or small, as it is in God,
in its sanctity and nobility,
for even something as little
as a flower, possessing
its being in God, is more
lovely and better than
the rest of the world
put together.
To know that little flower
is to be closer to God
than if you knew an angel.

Like Caterpillars in the Trees

God's pure being so draws us that,
small as we are—
like caterpillars who fall
from the trees and slowly
begin to make
their return
to that prior height—
we climb.
In that life
we see our lives,
in the brilliance
of the midday sun.

Experiencing God

If you are to experience God
truly, you will experience
God in all circumstances,
when all is well with you,
as well as when you stumble;
when you are in tears,
as well as in moments of joy.
God should be the same
for you in every circumstance,
and never should you confine
God to only one side of devotion.
God is not weeping or joyful, but
God is everything all at once
or nothing at all.

To Know God Truly

To know God truly is to know God
without any means.
Without senses.
Then, it is impossible to be fooled by
God-that-is-not-God.
A blinding like St. Paul experienced
on the road to Damascus—
when by seeing nothing the apostle
in fact met God—is what
every one of us needs.

Love of God

Love everything, here and everywhere,
that moves you closer to God. For if you
desired to see a foreign land by crossing
the sea, you would want a ship to carry you there.
But then having crossed the wide ocean, you would
no longer have need of a ship, even though
you loved it with the love of God,
because after loving a thing in such a way,
you turn inward again and say, with the Song,
My beloved is mine and I am his.

Self-Shedding

Hear this, because it is astonishing:
to come to God, to be in God,
is to be so transformed
as to shed one's self.
What was mine—wisdom,
reputation, even identity—
vanishes like old skin.
What is in God is God.
This soul is not even my own;
this soul is yours, God.
What soul?
May God so help us. Amen.

Amen

Why did God create the world and the angelic host,
and why were the glorious scriptures ever written?
Why, we might also ask, does anything exist at all?
The answers are both enormous and tidy in the extreme,
a mundane mingling with the holy in the most
extraordinary ways. It is simply because of this:
so that God might be born in the soul, so that
your soul might be born in God,
in order that you may utter
Amen.

Grace Is

Grace is a union with God, a holy indwelling
that performs no pious feats and does not work.
A holy union, grace is a delicate life of God-with-you,
of God-in-you; may it be so, and may no one
imagine this beyond their reach. With grace,
anything may happen, everything is possible,
and whatever comes along
on the road of life
is but a trifle.

We Shine

The light of God is like fire and flame shining
from above, from a sun that is too powerful
to withstand directly; no one could survive it,
but there is a place in each of us that is so clear
and noble that fire meets fire there, and it is in
that individual soul where we meet and live with
the Holy One. It is in that light that we shine.

Sources and Notes

The poems in this collection are not, strictly speaking, translations. They are, rather, *re-voicings* of Eckhart's thought that draw on key images, phrases, and ideas found in his writings. In one sense, of course, they do "translate" Eckhart, following the etymology of the Latin word *translatio*, which in late-medieval usage meant to "carry [something]" from one "place" to another (relics of saints were "translated," as medieval texts put it, from one place to another—e.g., to a monstrance, shrine, or altar). But these poems do this in a more expansive and creative sense than simply "moving" formulations found in Eckhart's original German or Latin into contemporary English.

As "re-voicings," these poems each found their inspiration in particular texts from Eckhart's writings as specified in the notes that follow. It is our intention, and hope, that these versions bring Eckhart's often complex and demanding formulations into succinct forms that remain true to his genius.

The notes that follow point to the specific sources lying behind each of the poems found in this collection. We do this to facilitate the interest of readers who might wish to pursue Eckhart's thought—as expressed in a given poem—in greater depth.

Sources

Clark, James M. and John V. Skinner, translators and editors, *Treatises and Sermons of Meister Eckhart*. New York: Harper and Brothers, 1958.

Davies, Oliver, editor and translator, *Meister Eckhart: Selected Writings*. New York: Penguin Books, 1994.

Quint, Josef, editor and translator. *Meister Eckhart, Werke, Vols. I and II*. Frankfurt am Main: Deutscher Klassiker Verlag, 1993.

Walshe, Maurice O'Connell, translator and editor, *The Complete Mystical Works of Meister Eckhart*, revised with a foreword by Bernard McGinn. Crossroad/Herder and Herder, 2009. This collection first appeared in a three-volume edition, with different pagination, as *Meister Eckhart. Sermons and Treatises*. Shaftesbury, Dorset: Element, 1987.

Abbreviations for Sources

TS   *Treatises and Sermons of Meister Eckhart.*

SW   *Selected Writings.*

MEW   *Meister Eckhart, Werke,* Vols. I and II.

CMW   *The Complete Mystical Works of Meister Eckhart.*

Note: The various editions of Eckhart number his sermons differently. Clark/Skinner, Davies, and Walshe do not agree in their numeration. Davies includes a "Register of the German Sermons" in an Appendix (273-6). A more expansive table is found in Walshe's 1987 edition (*Meister Eckhart. Sermons & Treatises,* 3 vols.) in an appendix entitled "Concordances" (Vol. 3, 150-60); this edition also includes a useful, though incomplete, index of the biblical texts, in this case limited to the single verse upon which Eckhart generally based his sermons Vol. 3, 161-7).

Notes

[in the order in which they appear]

Epigraphs: The first three quotations are from Meister Eckhart's treatise "On the Noble Man"; the last is from one of the German sermons as cited in the German edition translated by Josef Quinn, *Deutsche Predigten und Traktate*, 1963, 151 (our English translation).

Setting Forth Together. Draws on themes found throughout Eckhart's sermons and treatises, including the Apostle Paul's claim that "it is God who said, 'Let light shine out of darkness,' who has shone in our hearts . . . " (2 Cor. 4.6).

PART ONE: "IN THE BEGINNING . . . DARKNESS"

Want to Know How to Find God? From "The Talks of Instruction"; ch. 6; in SW, 18–9.

There Is a Light Within You. From German sermon 7, in SW, 133–35. The inner light Eckhart here speaks about is a theme found throughout his sermons and treatises; he calls it the "spark" or "little light" (*Fünklein*), which is the uncreated light of God that is found in every human soul.

Who You Are. From "The Talks of Instruction"; ch. 11; SW, 18–19.

The Darkness of Unknowing. From German sermon 25, referring to Luke 2.42; SW, 222–23.

Choose Darkness. From German sermon 25; in this sermon, Eckhart is commenting on Hosea 2.14; in SW, 222–25.

The Dark Way. From German sermon 4; CMW, 56.

Spoken in Solitude. From German sermon 4, with reference to Psalms 84.10; CMW, 57.

(*Sources for Poems on pp. ix–20*)

Obedience. From "The Talks of Instruction"; ch. 6; SW, 8–12.

Tasting Freedom. From "The Talks of Instruction"; ch. 1; SW, 3–4.

So You Can't Pray? From "The Talks of Instruction"; ch. 2; SW, 4–5.

Trying to Pray Properly. From "The Talks of Instruction"; ch. 1; SW, 3–4.

What's the Best Way to Find God? From "The Talks of Instruction"; ch. 6; SW, 8–9.

God Cannot Resist. From German sermon 7, in SW, 134.

Where Darkness Takes You. From "The Book of Divine Consolation"; Part II; TS, 118.

This Is Your Life. From "The Talks of Instruction"; ch. 7; SW, 12.

The Restlessness of Peace. From "The Talks of Instruction"; SW, 12–13.

There Is No Why. From German sermon 11 on John 4.23; CMW, 96.

Your Soul Has Two Faces. From German sermon 11 on John 4.23 with reference to ideas of Augustine and Avicenna; CMW, 96–97.

Will to do the good. From "The Talks of Instruction"; ch. 10; SW, 15.

Your Desire Matters. From "The Talks of Instruction"; SW, 16.

Religion Can Be a Trap. From "The Talks of Instruction"; SW, 17.

Go to the Desert. From "On the Noble Man" with a portion of Hosea 2.14; TS, 158–59.

Choose Silence. From German sermon 8, exploring Ephesians 5.8, "You were once in darkness . . . "; SW, 136–37.

You Are Not Alone. From "The Talks of Instruction"; ch. 11; SW, 20–21.

When You Are Seeking God. From "The Talks of Instruction"; ch. 6; SW, 18–19.

An Even Greater Marvel. From "The Talks of Instruction"; ch. 11; SW, 22.

The Need for Penance. From German sermon 4; CMW, 60.

God Is a God of the Present. From "The Talks of Instruction"; ch. 12; SW, 22–23.

What Does God See? From "The Talks of Instruction"; ch. 13; SW, 24.

Lighten Your Load. From "The Talks of Instruction"; ch. 15; SW, 25.

A Perfect Equation. From "The Talks of Instruction"; SW, 25–26.

In Such Company. From "The Book of Divine Consolation"; Part II; TS, 142.

Let God Be God in You. From "The Talks of Instruction"; ch. 16; SW, 26–27.

God Waits at Your Door. From "The Talks of Instruction"; ch. 17; SW, 28.

Whatever the Path. From "The Talks of Instruction"; SW, 29–30.

Love Is More Important. From "The Talks of Instruction"; SW, 29–30.

Letting Go of Getting It Right. From "The Talks of Instruction"; ch. 18; SW, 30–32.

You Are the Gift. From "The Talks of Instruction"; ch. 19; SW, 32–33.

Free Yourself of Your Self. From "The Talks of Instruction"; ch. 21; SW, 40–41.

Always in All Ways. From "The Talks of Instruction"; ch. 22; SW, 44–45.

Serenity and Service. From "The Talks of Instruction"; ch. 23; SW, 45–46.

Part Two: "Embracing Darkness"

Where Did You Come From? From German sermon 22 on Matthew 5.3, "Blessed are the poor in spirit"; SW, 204–05. Eckhart often refers to God— in God's "Godhead"—as "the eternal abyss of divine being," or elsewhere, as "the still desert." This is his way of speaking of the "God beyond God," which we cannot "know" in the way that we know other things.

In That Darkness. From German sermon 23 on John 16.16: "A little while, and you will see me no longer"; in SW, 209–10.

It Is Complicated. From "The Book of Divine Consolation"; Part I (end of the part); TS, 113–14.

If You Are Suffering. From "The Book of Divine Consolation"; Part I; TS, 113. This poem revalues Eckhart's teaching only in that the poem does not include his advice to stop loving "external things."

Bad Things and Good People. From "The Book of Divine Consolation"; TS, 113.

Giving Your Life for Justice. From "The Book of Divine Consolation"; TS, 112–13.

God Who Comforts. Opening paragraph and final sentence of "The Book of Divine Consolation." The reference to St. Paul is to 2 Corinthians 1.3; TS, 109, 148.

Goodness Cannot Be Born. From "The Book of Divine Consolation"; Part I; TS, 110.

You Must Free Yourself of Your Self. From German sermon 23 on John 16.16, "A little while, and you will see me no longer"; SW, 216–17.

The Best Way of All. From German sermon 22, on Matthew 5.3, the first of the Beatitudes: "Blessed are the poor in spirit"; SW, 206.

(Sources for Poems on pp. 50–57)

What You Have That Is Good. From "The Book of Divine Consolation"; Part I; TS, 110.

There Is So Much We Need. From "The Book of Divine Consolation"; TS, 110–11.

Consider Your Suffering. From "The Book of Divine Consolation"; Part III; TS, 147.

Child of God. From "The Book of Divine Consolation"; Part I; TS, 111, which reflects upon John 1.12–13.

God Is Near. From "The Book of Divine Consolation"; TS, 112. Eckhart says, "Assuredly all pain only comes from the fact that you do not turn to God and towards God alone."

Ask God to Free You of God. From German sermon 22, exploring Matthew 5.3, the first Beatitude: "Blessed are the poor in spirit"; SW, 203–04.

Much of Our Suffering. From "The Book of Divine Consolation"; Part I; TS, 112.

God Is Always Within You. From "On the Noble Man"; in SW, 102–03. Eckhart draws on the work of the theologian Origen who suggested that "the image of God, God's son, is in the ground of the soul like a spring of living water"; Eckhart expands upon this with reference to the story found in Genesis 26.15ff., which relates the story of Isaac digging up springs of living water. In this text as in so many others, Eckhart interprets the birth of the "Son" as archetypical for what awaits each person—for each of us is "to become God's only begotten Son."

Room Enough. From German sermon 22, on the first Beatitude, Matthew 5.3: "Blessed are the poor in spirit"; SW, 202–03.

(Sources for Poems on pp. 58–65)

One Love. From German sermon 9; Eckhart is commenting on two texts: "God loves the one who pursues justice" (Prov. 15.9) and "Blessed are those who hunger and thirst for justice" (Mt. 5.6); SW, 139–40.

Tend the Seed of God Within You. From "On the Noble Man"; Eckhart explores six stages of growth in "the inner person"; he prefaces this by commenting on one of Origen's Sermons on Genesis on God's planting "good seed" in our inner life, which "can never be destroyed or extinguished in itself, even if it is overgrown and hidden. [This seed] glows and gleams, shines and burns and always seeks God"; SW, 100–01.

Unholy Comfort. From "The Book of Divine Consolation"; Part II; TS, 114, with reference in the last two lines to Ecclesiasticus 11:27.

This Changes Everything. From "The Book of Divine Consolation"; in SW, 94–95.

God Has Not Left You. From "The Book of Divine Consolation"; Part II; TS, 116, with reference to Psalms 42.3.

Look Within Yourself for Truth. From "The Book of Divine Consolation"; in SW, 94–95.

Listen into the Wilderness. From German sermon 16, in SW, 175–6. Eckhart explores the text "Whoever hears me shall not be ashamed" (Ecclus. 24.30), giving voice to the theme that God is most truly found in what Eckhart calls "the abyss of his godhead"—or "the still desert" of God's "godhead." For this reason, we must "take leave of God for the sake of God," meaning abandon our conceptions of God for the truth that is beyond our knowing and naming—i.e., the godhead itself. This idea points to the "God beyond God" that is a common theme across theistic mystical traditions.

Listen to Seneca. From "The Book of Divine Consolation"; Part II; TS, 117.

The Rest You Desire. From German sermon 18, devoted to Luke 7.14, one of the healing stories in Luke's gospel, where Jesus commands a "young man" who had died: "Young man, I tell you: rise up"; SW, 186–87.

You Don't Know. From "The Book of Divine Consolation"; TS, 118.

The Heart's Desire. From "The Book of Divine Consolation"; TS, 116.

Who You Are. From "The Book of Divine Consolation"; Part II; TS, 119.

Your Home. From German sermon 4, on Luke 2.42; CMW, 55.

One of God's Consolations. From "The Book of Divine Consolation"; Part II; TS, 119–20.

Light Shines in Darkness. From "The Book of Divine Consolation"; Part II, with reference to John 1.5 and 2 Corinthians 12.9; TS, 121.

God's Promise. From "The Book of Divine Consolation"; Part II; TS, 122.

You Cannot Have Both. From "The Book of Divine Consolation"; Part II; TS, 122.

When in Darkness. From "The Book of Divine Consolation"; Part II, with reference to Matthew 5.3; TS, 123.

The Way to Consolation. From "The Book of Divine Consolation"; Part II; TS, 123.

So you want to find God? From "On the Noble Man"; in SW, 104–06.

Soul Arising. From "The Book of Divine Consolation"; Part II; TS, 123–24.

Remember Your Source. From "The Book of Divine Consolation"; TS, 124.

The Spark and the Fire. From "The Book of Divine Consolation"; TS, 124.

Gratitude. From "The Book of Divine Consolation"; TS, 127.

My Loss. From "The Book of Divine Consolation"; TS, 128.

Like a Stone. From "The Book of Divine Consolation"; TS, 129–30.

When You Are Bereft. From "The Book of Divine Consolation"; Part II, where Eckhart is citing Mark 1.11, the voice heard at Jesus's baptism; TS, 132.

Little by Little. From German sermon 16, an exploration of Ecclesiasticus 24.30: "Whoever hears me shall not be ashamed"; SW, 178.

Begotten Is Begetting. From "The Book of Divine Consolation"; Part II; TS, 134.

Nothing Else Matters. From German sermon 17, in SW, 180. Eckhart is commenting on Ephesians 4.6: "One God and Father of all, who is blessed above all and through all and in all." He sets this alongside Luke. 14.10, "Friend, climb up higher, draw higher," using the gospel text to speak of a presumed dialogue between God (who is speaking) and the soul (as the addressee).

God Draws Us. From "The Book of Divine Consolation"; Part II, with reference to Hosea 2.14; TS, 136.

Nothing–More Prayer. From "The Book of Divine Consolation"; Part II, with reference to Wisdom 7.11; TS, 139.

A Body That Suffers. From "The Book of Divine Consolation"; Part II, with reference to Acts of the Apostles 5.41; TS, 138.

Give Me Trouble. From "The Book of Divine Consolation"; Part II, with reference to Psalms 91.15; TS, 139.

God–Friend. From "The Book of Divine Consolation"; Part II; TS, 140.

PART THREE: "AWAKING TO LIGHT"

Where God's Radiance Dwells. From German sermon 8 on Ephesians 5.8: "Once you were in darkness, but now a light in the Lord"; SW, 136–37. In this sermon, Eckhart expounds his insight that that soul "flows forth" in the trinitarian procession—within God—by which certain medieval theologians argued that the Son and the Spirit flowed forth from the Father as what they called a "procession." What is extraordinary is that Eckhart locates the birth of each soul within that procession: "The Holy Spirit flowers from the work of God, from the birth in which the Father generates his only begotten Son and from this outflowing in such a way that it proceeds from them both and the soul flows forth in this procession."

You Say That You Cannot See. From German sermon 1, on Wisdom 18.14; CMW, 34.

Awakening to Light. From German sermon 19 on Acts of the Apostles 9:8 with reference to Song of Solomon 3.1: "Upon my bed at night I sought him whom my soul loves; I sought him, but found him not; I called him, but he gave no answer"; CMW, 137–39.

The Light of God. From German sermon 19 on Acts of the Apostles 9:8; CMW, 139.

You Will Have It. From German sermon 16 on Acts of the Apostles 1:4; CMW, 125.

Clear Water. From German sermon 16 on Acts of the Apostles 1:4; CMW, 125.

The Power of Practice. From "The Talks of Instruction"; ch. 6; SW, 12.

Christmas Is Today and Every Day. From "The Book of Divine Consolation"; in SW, 80–81. A recurring theme, that we are also to "give birth to the Son";

(Sources for Poems on pp.96–103)

sometimes Eckhart goes so far as to say that each of us should "become the only-begotten Son of God." See "God Is Always Within You" and the accompanying note on this theme.

Breaking-Through to Become Free of God. From German sermon 22, on the first of the Beatitudes; SW, 208–09. Here Eckhart cites his Dominican confrere, Albert the Great; it is possible that Eckhart had been his student, though this is unclear. Eckhart goes further than Albert had in asserting that the "poor person" Jesus was describing in this passage is one who "desires nothing, knows nothing, and possesses nothing." Before turning his full attention to his interpretation, he pauses to address his hearers: "I beseech you for the love of God to understand me if you can. But if you don't understand this truth, don't worry about it, for I shall be speaking of truth in a manner that only a few good people can understand." At stake is his conviction that only experience can ground us in understanding the truth; we do not arrive at an understanding of it through an abstract knowing that might lead to experience.

You Will Not See. From German sermon 1, on Wisdom 18.14; CMW, 34–35.

A Saving Equation. From German sermon 24 on Matthew 2.2, where we find the "wise men from the East" come to Jerusalem to ask King Herod: "Where is the one who is born King of the Jews?"; SW, 221. Eckhart is intent on reminding his hearers/readers that "this birth takes place in the soul just as it takes place in eternity, no more and no less. For there is only one birth, and this takes place in the essence and ground of the soul." See also, 215.

Little by Little. From German sermon 5 on Jeremiah 1.9–10: "The Lord stretched out his hand and touched my mouth and spoke to me"; SW, 127–28. Eckhart gives voice to one of his favorite themes, *Abgeschiedenheit*, which could be translated as "separation" or "isolation"—i.e., "aloneness"—where we become free of an attachment to things, people, and even our self. Not loneliness but freedom is what Eckhart is accentuating.

You Are the Cause of God. From German sermon 22, in which he comments on the first Beatitude, "Blessed are the poor in spirit"; SW, 207–08.

Free Yourself. From German sermon 5, on the text from Jeremiah 1. 9–10: "The Lord stretched out his hand and touched my mouth and spoke to me"; SW, 127. The verb Eckhart uses, rendered here as "in-formed," *einbilden*, has physicality; it could be understood as an "imagining" (since *Bild* in German means "picture" or "image") as an act of divine creativity.

Heaven Is Cheap. From German sermon 6, where Eckhart explores John 12.26, drawing on the theologian known as Dionysius, whom theologians in Eckhart's day still considered to be the philosopher converted by the preaching of the Apostle Paul (see Acts 17.16–34). Dionysius—or Pseudo-Dionysius as he is generally called today—was revered as a mystic throughout the Middle Ages. SW, 131–32.

Three Ways in God. From German sermon 21, on the story of Jesus's encounter with Mary and Martha. Eckhart develops his notion of "the wayless way, which is free and yet bound, in which we are raised and exalted above ourselves and all things, with neither will nor images, although not yet in substantial being." Eckhart expounds his approach in the line from that story (in Lk. 10.38): "Jesus entered a certain village where a woman named Martha received him." SW, 196–98.

Your Somethingness in God. From German sermon 6 on John 12.26: "Whoever serves me should follow me, and wherever I am, there should my servant also be"; SW, 132–33.

Peace Is Not Your Goal. From "The Talks of Instruction"; ch. 23; SW, 51.

Do Not Seek the Way. From German sermon 19 on 1 John. 4.9: "God's love was revealed to us in this, that [God] sent [God's] son into the world that we should live through him"; SW, 190–91.

Darkness Will Do. From German sermon 16 on Ecclesiasticus 24.30: "Whoever hears me shall not be ashamed"; SW, 175–77.

Filling What Is Empty. From German sermon 4; CMW, 58.

No Matter What. From "On the Noble Man"; SW, 103. The text Eckhart cites is from John 1.5: "The light shines in the darkness, and the darkness did not overcome it."

Why worry about growing old? From German sermon 18, exploring Jesus's healing of the "young man" presumed to be dead whom he commanded to "rise up"; SW, 185–86.

Pouring In. From German sermon 4, with reference to Revelation 3.20; CMW, 58.

Heaven Refuses to Keep a Distance. From German sermon 7, in SW, 133–34.

The Rest You Desire. From German sermon 19 on 1 John 4.9; SW, 190.

Always Be Ready for the Miracle. From German sermon 2 on Luke 1. 26,28: "At that time the angel Gabriel was sent by God . . . "; SW, 118.

More God than I Am Myself. From German sermon 19 on 1 John 4.9; he refers here to Augustine's treatise "On the Epistle of John" tr. 2, n. 14; SW, 188–89.

Your True Beauty. From German sermon 30, in which Eckhart wonders what it means that we should "Seek first the kingdom of God" (Lk. 12.31), and draws on the Song of Songs 1.8: "Do you not know yourself, most beautiful of women? Go out, then, and follow in the footsteps of your lord"; in SW, 243, 248–49.

God Sees No Sin. From German sermon 19 on 1 John 4.9; SW, 188–89.

The One Needful Thing. From German sermon 30; SW, 250–51. See also the note above on "Your True Beauty."

There God Shines. From German sermon 18, exploring Jesus's healing of the "young man" who had died, whom he charges to "rise up!" (Lk. 7.14); SW, 184–85.

Becoming a New Creation. From German sermon 2 on Luke 1.26,28; SW, 117.

What About You? From German sermon 17 on Ephesians 4.6, "One God and Father of all . . . "; SW, 183–84.

God Delights in You as God. From German sermon 27 on Matthew 10.28: "Do not fear those who would kill the body, for they cannot kill the soul"; SW, 233.

To Love as God Loves. From German sermon 16 on Ecclesiasticus 24.30, with reference to the "Great Command" in Matthew 22.39; SW, 176.

Make the Best of Everything. From German sermon 4 on 2 Timothy 4.2,5), which the Vulgate renders as "Preach the word vigilantly, with great effort"; Eckhart renders this verse as "Speak the word, spread it out, bring it forth and give birth to the word"; SW, 125–26.

Learn to Rest. From German sermon 10 on Wisdom 5.16: "The just shall live in eternity, and their reward is with the Lord"; SW, 147–48. Here, as elsewhere in his writings, Eckhart explores the ancient Christian teaching that God created *ex nihilo*, or "out of nothing"; this is the reason why he argues that we must become *nichts*, or "nothing," so that God can make us "something" (*etwas*)—and, in this, God differs from creatures, who can only make "something" from "something."

Obedience Isn't What You Think. From "The Talks of Instruction"; ch. 1; SW, 3–4.

What is the Hardest Thing of All? From German sermon 16 on Ecclesiasticus 24.30, "Whoever hears me shall not be ashamed"; SW, 176.

(Sources for Poems on pp. 126–134)

Breaking-Through. From German sermon 27 on the text from Matthew 10.28; SW, 234–35.

What Is a Free Mind? From "The Talks of Instruction"; ch. 2; SW, 4–5.

Looking in All the Wrong Places. From "The Talks of Instruction"; ch. 3; SW, 5–7. Eckhart cites St. Peter's claim in Matthew 19.27: "See, Lord, we have left everything."

You Are the Gift. From "The Talks of Instruction"; ch. 3; SW, 5–7.

Everything Is God. From German sermon 16 on Ecclesiasticus 24.30, "Whoever hears me shall not be ashamed"; SW, 178. Eckhart voices his notion of what he calls the "Godhead" (*Gottheit*), which some commentators have rendered the "God beyond God"—but it could also be conceived of as "God-ness." The phrase "the abyss of God's Godness" is Eckhart's way of saying that nothing within us can comprehend the essential nature of the divine, though he also—and often—insists that we always carry within us an "image" in the "little spark" of uncreated light, which is God.

It's Not About You. From "The Talks of Instruction"; ch. 5; SW, 8.

The Waking Heart. From German sermon 4 on 2 Timothy 4.2,5; SW, 124–25. Eckhart cites from Song of Solomon 5.2, "I slept, but my heart is awake," a passage that had a celebrated history in medieval commentaries as an explanation of mystical experience—in which one enjoys the "depths" of God's presence, as if asleep, while one's heart remains awake. Eckhart's translation of the German phrase *mein Herz wacht* could be rendered, in English, either as "my heart is awake" or as "my heart keeps watch."

Everything Will Become God. From "The Talks of Instruction"; ch. 6; SW, 8–11.

Everything and Everywhere. From "The Talks of Instruction"; ch. 3; SW, 5–7; SW, 9–12.

The Spark Within You. From German sermon 10 on Wisdom. 5.16, "The just one lives in eternity; SW, 144. Eckhart could have no idea about our modern psychological sense of the "ego," first articulated by Freud before becoming part of our common vocabulary. But he did insist that "ego" could only properly be used to speak of God, arguing that "'Ego,' the Latin word for 'I', can be used properly by God alone in [God's] unity." See, for instance, German sermon 3 in SW, 122.

Tasting God in Everything. From "The Talks of Instruction"; ch. 3; SW, 5–7; SW, 9–11.

The Rest Will Follow. From German sermon 30; SW, 242–43; see the note above on "Your True Beauty."

There Is Only One Birth. From German sermon 23 on John. 16.16: "A little while and you will see me no more"; SW, 216–17.

A Matter of the Heart. From "The Talks of Instruction"; ch. 6; SW, 9–10.

The Hardest Truth. From German sermon 30; SW, 243–45; see the note above on the poem "Your True Beauty."

Part Four: "Living in Radiance"

You Carry an Inner Radiance. From German sermon 5, on Jeremiah 1.9–10: "The Lord stretched out his hand and touched my mouth and spoke to me"; SW, 127–8. Eckhart voices his conviction that each of us carries a "little spark" (or *Fünklein*) within us, which is the uncreated light of God which no darkness—not ours or any other—can overcome.

Learn to Break-Through Things. From "The Talks of Instruction"; ch. 6; SW, 10–11.

Restlessness and Radiance. From "The Talks of Instruction"; ch. 6; SW, 10–11.

There Is No Death. From Latin sermon on Luke 16.1–9; TS, 199.

Savoring God. From Latin sermon on Luke 10.23–37; TS, 220.

You Are a Desert. From German sermon 3, with reference to Matthew 3.3; CMW, 52.

You Are a Construction Zone. From German sermon 4 on 2 Timothy 4.2,5: "Preach the word, vigilantly, and with great exertion"; SW, 123. See also the note accompanying "Make the Best of Everything," above.

Don't Do Too Much. From German sermon 3; CMW, 52.

Ridiculous Joy. From German sermon 16 on Ecclesiasticus 24.30: "Whoever hears me will not be ashamed"; SW, 178.

Virtue Shines Out, Day and Night. From *The Book of Divine Consolation*; ch. 2; SW, 75–76. Here Eckhart writes that through the "inner work" of virtue our life "shines and illuminates, both day and night," adding that actions rather than words fulfill the biblical mandate to "sing to the Lord a new song" (Ps. 95.1). What matters is not the "outer" work of virtue, but the "inner work" that arises from the "radiant" soul.

Everything Is One in God. From German sermon 16 on Ecclesiasticus 24.30: "Whoever hears me shall not be ashamed"; SW, 177–78. Eckhart's example of the fly as greater than "the highest angel" would have shocked and probably offended his first hearers; it may do the same today.

You and God. From German sermon 16 on Acts of the Apostles 1.4; CMW, 126–27.

Asleep to Things. From German sermon 18 on 2 Timothy 4.2 with reference to "the Lord's prayer" in Matthew 6.10 and Song of Songs 5.2; CMW, 134.

Crying in the Wilderness. From Latin sermon on Luke 16.1–9, with reference to Luke 3.4; TS, 199.

A Thousand Times More. From German sermon 4; CMW, 56.

When You Have Nothing. From Latin sermon on Luke 16.1–9, with reference to a homily of St. Chrysostom and John 14.6; TS, 202.

Open Your Self to the Radiance. From German sermon 7, in SW, 135–36. In this sermon, Eckhart explores a common theme, his notion of the "little spark" found in every human soul; see the note to "There Is a Light Within You" above. This is one of his few sermons without any biblical references, based as it is on a disputed question in the "schools"; Eckhart cites two authorities here: the Jewish philosopher Maimonides and his treatise *The Guide for the Perplexed,* and then Aristotle's *On the Heavens.* See also, "Listen to Seneca" in this volume. As Eckhart might have put it, "truth is truth" irrespective of its origin or authorship.

Light Is for the Humble. From Latin sermon on Luke 16.1–9, with reference to Psalms 36.9, Psalms 4.6, and Exodus 33.20; TS, 204–05.

Stop Your Seeking. From German sermon 4; CMW, 58.

I Can't Feel God. From German sermon 4, with reference to John 3.8; CMW, 58–59.

When You Are Empty. From German sermon 4; CMW, 59.

This Birth of God in Me. From German sermon 4; CMW, 59.

Breaking-Through Things. From "The Talks of Instruction"; ch. 6; SW, 10–11. The notion of "breaking through" (durchbrechen) is central to Eckhart's thinking, and a word he coined in his vernacular German writings; here, he puts it this way: "We must learn to break through things and grasp God by this means, so that we allow God to take form substantially and powerfully within us." One of the images of God that Eckhart frequently used is that of the "still desert."

Prayer for the Birth of God. From German sermon 4; CMW, 59.

Fishhook-Love. From German sermon 4; CMW, 60.

To Meet God Alone. From Latin sermon on Luke 16.1–9; TS, 207.

You Really Are. From Latin sermon on Luke 16.1–9; TS, 201.

Identity Crisis. From German sermon 6 on Matthew 21.12; CMW, 66.

Clinging. From Latin sermon on Luke. 16.1–9, with reference to James 2.5; TS, 201–02.

Clearing the Temple. From German sermon 6 on Matthew 21.12; CMW, 69.

You Will See Again. From German sermon 7 on 1 John 3.1, with reference to John. 16.22; CMW, 72.

A Spark from the Fire. From Latin sermon on Luke 10.23–37; TS, 216–17.

Divine Fruit. From Latin sermon on Luke 10.23–37, with reference to Confessions 1,1.5; TS, 220.

How Iron Puts on Fire. From Latin sermon on Romans 13.11–14, with reference to Romans. 13.12; TS, 221.

Beware of the Good People. From German sermon 9 on Luke 10.38 with reference to Matthew 26.38; CMW, 88.

Whatever Happens. From "On the Noble Man"; TS, 158.

Love for Nothing. From German sermon 12 on John. 15.12; CMW, 100.

Make Me Less. From German sermon 12 on John 15.12 with reference to Matthew 6.10; CMW, 100. *Paternoster* ("Our Father" in Latin) is the way people in Eckhart's day referred to this prayer.

Stay Inside. From German sermon 13(b) on 1 John 4.9; CMW, 111.

How to Love This World. From German sermon 14 on Hebrews 11.37; SW, 166.

Like Caterpillars in the Trees. From German sermon 14 on Hebrews 11.37; SW, 166–67.

Experiencing God. From German sermon 19 on 1 John 4.9; SW, 190–91.

To Know God Truly. From German sermon 19 on Acts of the Apostles 9.8; CMW, 141.

Love of God. From German sermon 26 on Revelation 21.2 with reference to Song of Solomon 2.16; CMW, 170.

Self-Shedding. From German sermon 25 on Acts of the Apostles 12.11; CMW, 167.

(Sources for Poems on pp. 179–189)

Amen. From German sermon 29 on Luke 1.26,28; CMW, 177.

Grace Is. From German sermon 29 on Luke 1.26,28; CMW, 181.

We Shine. From German sermon 30 on Matthew 16.17; CMW, 184–85.

INDEX TO POEMS

ABOUT THE AUTHORS

Jon M. Sweeney

PHOTO BY MAURY WOLL

Jon M. Sweeney is an award-winning author and independent scholar who has been interviewed in print by a range of publications from the *Dallas Morning News* to *the Irish Catholic*, and on television for *CBS Saturday Morning* and many other programs.

His book, *The Pope Who Quit* (2014) has sold over 60,000 copies and was optioned by HBO. Jon is also the author of forty other books on spirituality, mysticism, and religion, including books about Francis of Assisi and Franciscan spirituality that have sold more than 200,000 copies; several biographies including one on the author of *Black Elk Speaks* titled *Nicholas Black Elk: Medicine Man, Catechist, Saint* and, more recently, *Thomas Merton: An Introduction to His Life and Practices*, published by St. Martins Essentials and Penguin Random House Audio in 2021.

In the late 1990s, Jon cofounded a multifaith publishing house, SkyLight Paths Publishing, in Vermont. Today, he still works in books, and speaks regularly at literary and religious conferences. Jon is a Catholic married to a rabbi, and their inter-faith marriage has been profiled in national media. He's active on social media (Twitter @jonmsweeney; Facebook jonmsweeney) and lives in Milwaukee.

Mark S. Burrows

PHOTO BY EMMA BURROWS

After almost a decade of university teaching in Germany, the capstone to a career spanning four decades as scholar and teacher in the US and Europe, Burrows returned to the US in 2020, and now lives by the sea in Camden, Maine. The focus of his scholarly work explores the intersection of spirituality and the arts, mysticism, and poetics. He also travels widely throughout the US, Europe and the UK, and Australia, lecturing and offering retreats and workshops on spirituality, poetics, and mysticism.

As a poet, Burrows writes with what Jay Parini recently described as "a profound awareness of nature and its spiritual resonances," and Christine Valters Paintner speaks of his poems as "treasures [that] lay themselves out like a banquet for the heart." His recent collection, *The Chance of Home: Poems*, appeared in 2018. A winner of the Wytter Bynner Prize in Poetry and numerous nominations for a Pushcart Prize, his poems have appeared in more than thirty journals in the US, Europe, Australia, and Asia. He also edits poetry for the academic journal *Spiritus* and is poetry editor for Wildhouse Publications.

His work as a translator of German poetry led to the award-winning publication of Rainer Maria Rilke's *Prayers of a Young Poet* (2012), the original version of poems that became the opening section of *The Book of Hours*. He also published *99 Psalms*, a collection of German poems by the Iranian-German poet, SAID (2013), as well as the first collection, in English translation, of poems by the German-Jewish writer Hilde Domin, *The Wandering Radiance* (2023).

He lives and writes in Camden, Maine. Visit him at *www. msburrows.com.*

HAMPTON ROADS PUBLISHING COMPANY
. . . for the evolving human spirit

Hampton Roads Publishing Company publishes books on a
variety of subjects, including spirituality, health, and other
related topics.

For a copy of our latest trade catalog, call (978) 465-0504
or visit our distributor's website at *www.redwheelweiser.com*. You
can also sign up for our newsletter and special offers by going to
www.redwheelweiser.com/newsletter/.